Action Research for Classrooms, Schools, and Communities

Action Research for Classrooms, Schools, and Communities

Meghan McGlinn Manfra

Los Angeles | London | New Delhi
Singapore | Washington DC | Melbourne

FOR INFORMATION:

SAGE Publications, Inc.
2455 Teller Road
Thousand Oaks, California 91320
E-mail: order@sagepub.com

SAGE Publications Ltd.
1 Oliver's Yard
55 City Road
London, EC1Y 1SP
United Kingdom

SAGE Publications India Pvt. Ltd.
B 1/I 1 Mohan Cooperative Industrial Area
Mathura Road, New Delhi 110 044
India

SAGE Publications Asia-Pacific Pte. Ltd.
18 Cross Street #10-10/11/12
China Square Central
Singapore 048423

Copyright © 2021 by SAGE Publications, Inc.

All rights reserved. Except as permitted by U.S. copyright law, no part of this work may be reproduced or distributed in any form or by any means, or stored in a database or retrieval system, without permission in writing from the publisher.

All third-party trademarks referenced or depicted herein are included solely for the purpose of illustration and are the property of their respective owners. Reference to these trademarks in no way indicates any relationship with, or endorsement by, the trademark owner.

Printed in the United States of America

Library of Congress Cataloging-in-Publication Data

Names: Manfra, Meghan McGlinn, author.

Title: Action research for classrooms, schools, and communities / Meghan McGlinn Manfra.

Description: Thousand Oaks, California : SAGE Publications, Inc, 2020. | Includes bibliographical references.

Identifiers: LCCN 2019030297 | ISBN 9781506316048 (paperback) | ISBN 9781506316062 (epub) | ISBN 9781506316055 (epub) | ISBN 9781506316031 (ebook)

Subjects: LCSH: Action research in education—Methodology.

Classification: LCC LB1028.24 .M384 2020 | DDC 370.72—dc23

LC record available at https://lccn.loc.gov/2019030297

This book is printed on acid-free paper.

Acquisitions Editor: Steve Scoble
Editorial Assistant: Elizabeth You
Production Editor: Kelle Clarke
Copy Editor: Terri Lee Paulsen
Typesetter: Hurix Digital
Proofreader: Sarah J. Duffy
Indexer: Judy Hunt
Cover Designer: Ginkhan Siam
Marketing Manager: Jillian Ragusa

20 21 22 23 24 10 9 8 7 6 5 4 3 2 1

Brief Contents

Detailed Contents

PART III COLLECTING AND ANALYZING DATA

PART IV   SHARING FINDINGS

Preface

∙∙∙

When Marilyn Cochran-Smith and Susan Lytle (1999) traced a decade of the action research movement in American educational research, they pointed to five major trends—the growing prominence of teacher action research, the emergence of theoretical or conceptual frameworks to describe action research, the dissemination of findings from action research beyond local audiences, the emergence of critiques of action research, and the discussion of the transformative potential of action research. Their article appeared at a time of increasing acceptance that action research could transform teacher education and shape school improvement reform. They wrote:

> The direction of the movement in the years to come is uncertain. . . . Its history so far would suggest, however, that some of the ideas that are central to the movement are deeply compelling to teachers, teacher educators, researchers, and others who have worked collectively to improve the school lives and life chances of students—and thus are likely to be sustained. (p. 22)

They could hardly have anticipated the dramatic swing in educational reform that has challenged the ability of teacher educators, practitioners, and educational researchers to sustain the action research movement. Beginning with No Child Left Behind in 2001 and continued through Race to the Top (2009) and the reauthorization of the Every Student Succeeds Act (ESSA, 2015), today educational research is most often conducted by outside researchers as experimental or quasi-experimental studies. The "research-based" approach to educational reform dominates policy and practice conversations in American education, especially related to high-stakes testing and curriculum standardization. For example, most states in the United States assign public schools with letter grades to indicate school performance based on achievement test scores and growth measures. Low-performing schools risk being taken over by the state. Added to this, there is a marked trend toward the continued deprofessionalization of teachers and teacher educators and an emphasis on market-based approaches to schooling. Today, the professional preparation of preservice teachers is also punctuated by high-stakes testing and assessments, including edTPA.

The result of this narrow, top-down approach to school reform within the educational research community has been to separate educational research scientists from practitioners—those responsible for the day-to-day work of schooling. At the same time, there are concerns about a divide between research and practice and it is common to read about complex professional development programs designed to encourage teachers to adopt "best practices." Rarely do we challenge contemporary approaches to education reform. Rather, the burden is placed on practitioners to pick up "what works" from researchers and put it into practice. There is little to suggest within this model that educational researchers should engage practitioners as part of the research enterprise, first seeking to understand daily issues related to practice and then working to bring about change.

This text, *Action Research for Classrooms, Schools, and Communities*, seeks to revive the spirit of action research and highlight areas of growth and potential. I build on previous work focused on action research to offer a new approach for considering educational research and school reform. Rather than continue to pursue top-down, one-size-fits-all models, action research provides a systematic and intentional approach to changing classrooms, schools, and communities. When educators pursue action research as a methodology, they honor the work of practitioners and value insider knowledge or "craft knowledge" about educational issues. This methodology embraces a constructivist epistemological lens that rejects knowledge creation as separate from experience or actual practice. Rather, the aim within action research is to contribute to the scholarship about what works in education by engaging in inquiry through action.

I was first introduced to this methodology as a teacher when I conducted my first action research study about the efficacy of using Webquests with my high school students. Later, in graduate school, I worked with teacher educators who integrated action research as a major part of their graduate courses. Working with experienced teachers I witnessed firsthand the tremendous impact of action research on teaching. They pursued questions very tightly connected to practice. As a result of their work, they improved their pedagogical content knowledge and became advocates for their students. These early experiences have led me to continue to study the benefits of action research, especially as a professional learning opportunity for teachers. This book reflects much of my experience working with experienced teachers and doctoral students, teaching courses on action research at the university level.

The overall aim of *Action Research for Classrooms, Schools, and Communities* is to provide a comprehensive overview of action research as an educational research methodology. In order to do this, I synthesize across a wide variety of relevant action research literature to provide background about the methodology, including its theoretical basis. I present action research as a response to contemporary educational reform, engaging practitioners across the educational ecology—within classrooms, schools, and the wider community—to bring about change. I provide a step-by-step approach for conducting action research, including framing a study, posing research questions, collecting and analyzing data, and disseminating the results.

Intended Audience

This book is primarily designed for educators, although other practitioners will benefit from the more general aspects of action research described here. Both novice and experienced researchers will learn about strategies associated with planning, conducting, and reporting action research studies. Readers will have access to both practical and theoretical discussions about action research as a methodology. This text would be appropriate for both preservice and experienced teachers as well as students enrolled in graduate education programs. Educational leaders and policy makers will also learn about the benefits of action research through this book.

Major Features

The text is organized around the four main sections focused on answering the call to action, planning action research studies, collecting and analyzing data, and sharing findings. Across these four sections, I trace relevant aspects of the action research cycle—problem posing, action, observation, reflection, and sharing (see Figure P.1).

It is important to note that action research methodology is recursive. The five steps in the cycle are often repeated, and you may engage in these steps simultaneously and several times across a project. For example, as you begin to frame your action research questions (*problem posing*), you will need to review relevant research literature, reflect on the literature, and then develop action research questions. As you begin to collect data to pursue a problem, you will initiate an action step, while also observing (*collecting data*) and reflecting (*analyzing data*) on the effects of that action. Figure P.2 provides an illustration of the overlapping, recursive nature of action research.

Organization of Text

This text is organized into three main parts: Part I focuses on "Answering the Call to Action," Part II focuses on "Planning an Action Research Study," Part III provides strategies for "Collecting and Analyzing Data," and Part IV focuses on "Sharing Findings."

Part I begins with Chapter 1, "Action Research in Contemporary Contexts," which provides readers with a working definition of action research and the rationale for pursuing this methodology to solve both practical and critical issues facing educational practitioners. This chapter places action research within the context of contemporary school reform and explores the relevance of systems theory for approaching action research across complex educational systems. Ultimately, the focus is on encouraging practitioners to work for change through reflection in action. In Chapter 2, "Approaches to Action Research," practitioners are invited to explore issues related to practice by conducting a gap analysis and/or needs assessment. An important focus of this chapter is learning to frame problems that reflect your educational values and worldview.

Part II provides guidance for planning an action research study. This begins in Chapter 3, "Literature Review and Theoretical Frameworks," by analyzing relevant research literature and evaluating the appropriateness of a priori theory to frame your action research study. Suggestions for using technology to enhance your search are offered. The aim here is for action research to be generative—to build on previous work—while also reflecting the specific needs and concerns of the action researcher conducting the study. In Chapter 4, "Research Questions and Ethics," action researchers build on their review of the literature to develop research questions. Guidance is offered for appropriately framing your study to make it not only logistically feasible but also ethical for your participants.

Part III focuses on collecting and analyzing data. This section takes a familiar approach to discussing social science research by discussing strategies for collecting

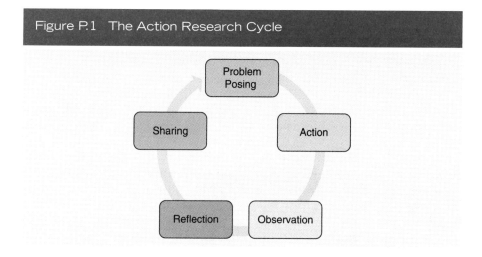

Figure P.1   The Action Research Cycle

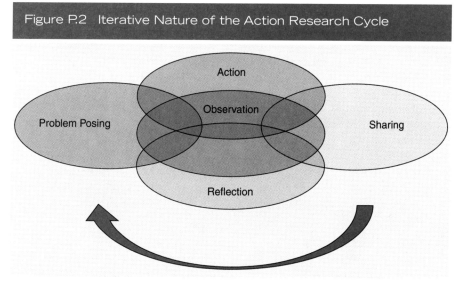

Figure P.2   Iterative Nature of the Action Research Cycle

and analyzing both quantitative and qualitative data. Qualitative approaches to educational research are emphasized since these approaches seem to align most naturally to the constructivist paradigm from which action research originates. Nonetheless, quantitative data can be incredibly useful and compelling for action researchers, and mixed methods approaches may be particularly fruitful for action researchers.

Chapter 5, "Qualitative Approaches to Data Collection," focuses mainly on the big three of qualitative data collection: interviews, observation, and archival data. I provide step-by-step directions for conducting both one-to-one interviews and focus groups, gathering field notes through observation, and conducting unobtrusive approaches to data collection by gathering documents, artifacts, and student or teacher work samples. In addition to these traditional approaches to qualitative data collection, the chapter also explores visual techniques, including photovoice and digital storytelling. The emphasis here is on triangulating data collection by collecting data from a variety of sources. Chapter 5 also includes "Shortcuts for Qualitative Data Collection in Action Research or Mini-Study" for practitioners who are interested in collecting data related to practice but, for logistical or ethical reasons, cannot conduct a full study.

Chapter 6, "Understanding Through Qualitative Data Analysis," provides detailed procedures for qualitative data analysis with a focus on inductive coding techniques. The chapter includes a discussion about data management and methods for using qualitative data analysis software (QDAS) to support the work of action researchers. It is important to note that rather than focus on reliability or generalizability, I focus on validity as a product of the trustworthiness of the study. I discuss strategies for improving trustworthiness, including working with critical friends and using member checks. The chapter includes "Shortcuts for Qualitative Data Analysis in Action Research or Mini-Study" for practitioners interested in analyzing data related to their practice but who do not have the time or opportunity to pursue a complete study.

Chapter 7, "Quantitative Approaches to Data Collection and Analysis," explores quantitative approaches that may be useful to action researchers. These include working with standardized assessment data, teacher-created assessments, and surveys and questionnaires. It also provides strategies for conducting mixed methods action research studies in which quantitative data inform qualitative data collection or qualitative data collection leads to quantitative research.

The final section, Part IV, "Sharing Findings," has one chapter—Chapter 8, "Reflection and the Action Research Report." The aim of this chapter is to provide encouragement and support for action researchers to share the findings of their action research with a larger audience. I emphasize that writing can provide a useful approach to data analysis and reflection. I also outline a step-by-step guide for writing an action research report. Finally, the chapter includes suggestions for exploring other avenues for disseminating research findings, including at conferences and through social media or other Web 2.0 technologies.

Pedagogical Aids

Throughout the text, pedagogical aids are offered to scaffold student learning and to prompt deeper thinking about the topics discussed. Each chapter begins with guiding questions and a list of terms. Within the text, I highlight key concepts using a variety of anecdotes, figures, and tables. At the end of each chapter, I include a list of reflection questions. These questions are designed to model reflective inquiry and can be used by instructors to assess student comprehension. Each chapter also includes a series of hands-on activities that I have used in my courses. These activities provide students with experiential learning opportunities and are designed to extend the chapters. As mentioned above, there are also shortcuts for conducting shortened versions of action research studies within the chapters on data collection and analysis. This will provide practitioners with a condensed approach to engaging in reflective inquiry when it is not feasible to conduct a full action research study.

Acknowledgments

I am grateful for the support I receive as an associate professor at North Carolina State University, especially from my graduate research assistants, Casey Holmes, Charlotte Roberts, and Jeff Greiner. I also owe a special thank-you to our media center faculty and staff, including Kerri Brown-Parker, who supported my research for this book. A special thank-you to my students at NC State, where I have taught several courses about action research over the years. Their feedback and experiences help to frame much of my thinking about action research and helped me identify issues and concerns that I find missing in other action research texts.

In 2010 I was able to visit the University of East Anglia, the former home of the Centre for Applied Research in Education (CARE), first started by Lawrence Stenhouse. Dr. Anna Robinson-Pant generously provided both her time and insights about action research and its evolution.

This book was inspired by the outstanding teacher educators that I worked with as a doctoral student at the University of North Carolina at Chapel Hill, including Drs. Dwight Rogers, Alan Tom, and Cheryl Bolick. My experiences as a teaching assistant and student in their courses influenced my future work as an action researcher.

I would also like to thank Nathan Davidson and Steve Scoble at Sage for their support of the development of this text.

Finally, a special thank-you to my family, especially Dennis, Mia, and Annabelle, for their continued love and support.

I hope this book helps to positively shape the educational experiences of all children. Through action research, we can become students of our students, making schooling more responsive to their needs.

SAGE and the author would like to thank the following reviewers for their feedback:

Valerie A. Allison, Susquehanna University

Tamarah M. Ashton, California State University, Northridge

Ann Bender, Marian University

Ann Bassett Berry, Plymouth State University

Steven P. Camicia, Utah State University

Elizabeth D. Cramer, Florida International University

Alicia R. Crowe, Kent State University

Gabrielle Kowalski, Cardinal Stritch University

Joellen Maples, St. John Fisher College

Ochieng' O. K'Olewe, McDaniel College

Craig Resta, Kent State University

Greer M. Richardson, La Salle University

Simon Saba, Centenary University

Dennis Stetter, Nova Southeastern University

Cheryl A. Franklin Torrez, The University of New Mexico

Susan A. Turner, Utah State University

Lynne Masel Walters, Texas A&M University

Regina M. Williams, Miami Dade College

Joy F. Xin, Rowan University

Answering the Call to Action

CHAPTER 1

Action Research in Contemporary Contexts

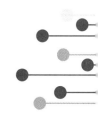

Guiding Questions

1. What are issues related to practice that you are passionately interested in learning more about?
2. What is action research? How has it been defined, and what are the main features of this methodology?
3. How can educational issues span multiple layers of the educational system? How might action researchers begin to tease these issues apart?

Keywords and Glossary

Action research: a research method for systematically and intentionally studying issues related to practice. It follows a cycle that includes problem posing, action, observation, reflection, and sharing.

Action research cycle: the cyclical approach to action research and the manner in which it follows a series of steps, each building on the previous and leading to the next.

Craft knowledge: the everyday knowledge about practice that teachers and other practitioners use to guide decision-making.

Reflection in action: the process of intentionally engaging in reflection about practice both during the active phase of practice (reflection in action) and before or during (reflection on action).

Systems theory: when applied to action research, promotes the inclusion of all stakeholders in the design of effective educational systems and the recognition that stakeholder participation is necessary to bring about change within educational systems.

Defining Action Research

How do you know that you are an effective practitioner? How do you know that you are making a positive impact on the students, teachers, or colleagues you work with each day? What are ways that you can improve your practice? There are many personal and professional benefits of reflective practice, and **action research** can be a powerful tool for engaging in this work.

Action research methodology follows a systematic and intentional cycle of problem posing, action, observation, reflection, and sharing. Action researchers ask and answer questions that emerge from issues related to everyday practice. This approach effectively flips the typical top-down approach to educational reform to provide a new space for practitioners, empowering them to bring about change across educational systems.

This book introduces action research methodology, including the history of action research and ways it has been used to address issues relevant to education reform. Each chapter will introduce you to various aspects of action research, including strategies for initiating a study, methods for collecting and analyzing data, and opportunities for sharing findings. We will begin by exploring the relevance of action research to contemporary school reform and then strategies action researchers can use to change their practice.

Action Research and the Context of Contemporary School Reform

The passage of the No Child Left Behind Act (NCLB) in 2001 ushered in a new phase in educational policy, with increased federal and state control of curriculum and instruction and high-stakes testing (Nichols, Glass, & Berliner, 2005). To some, NCLB marked another event in a long history of social efficiency in education, further eroding the professionalism of teachers, principals, and teacher educators through its mandates (e.g., Apple, 2005). Educational policy in the United States since the 1980s has increasingly focused on top-down reform measures designed to evaluate teacher performance and student growth (Eisner, 1992).

Contemporary teachers are buffeted by increasing oversight into their daily work. This includes a continued push by educational "reformers" to use student test scores on standardized tests and other value-added measures to account for teacher effectiveness. This age of accountability and high-stakes testing impacts teacher autonomy, professionalism, and decision-making. Yet practitioners everywhere know the truth: Each day thoughtful, reflective educators enter their classrooms or schools planning to positively impact the well-being and knowledge of their students. It is in this space of practice—the day-to-day activity of classrooms and schools—that learning occurs and, many would argue, where the real joy of teaching exists. Teachers matter. They make a difference in the lives of their students, and their relationships with students transcend professional concerns to include the nourishment and care of young people (Noddings, 1996).

Action research provides a structure or framework for teachers and other educational practitioners to study issues of importance related to educational practice. Unlike current top-down educational reform initiatives, it provides a space for practitioners to become the decision makers and knowledge creators—to effectively respond to contemporary educational contexts. Action research provides an opportunity for practitioners to make sense of educational policies within real classrooms and school settings. Rather than passively consume educational research conducted by an outside "other," in action research, practitioners make the decisions about the scope and direction of the research. They collect and analyze data, and draw and share conclusions. By making their insider knowledge public, action researchers contribute to the general knowledge base while also honing their own expertise. Whereas much of contemporary educational reform attempts to define the narrative for teachers and other practitioners, action research provides an opportunity for practitioners to add their insights about persistent issues related to educational practice.

What is Action Research?

For us, not officials.

Complex Educational Systems

Although research demonstrates that teachers are one of the most significant factors in student achievement (Rand Education, 2012; Rockoff, 2003), we also know that teachers do not act alone. Teachers act as "curricular-instructional gatekeepers" (Thornton, 2001) and are part of complex educational systems that include other teachers, school leaders, community members, and, of course, their students. A study of personal practice often evolves to become a study of these networks and the extent to which the system is healthy and supportive of student growth. Figure 1.1 illustrates the multiple layers of a typical education system in the United States.

The center of the educational system in this case is the classroom. Here, factors such as teacher background and experience, teacher philosophy and worldview, instructional strategies, curriculum resources, and the students themselves, with their own special talents, interests, needs and outcomes, impact the day-to-day life of classroom practice. However, classrooms do not exist in a vacuum. Rather, they are impacted by social, political, cultural, and economic factors often beyond the control of individual teachers and their students.

classrooms are impacted by politics and side factors

At the school level there are a variety of factors that impact classroom practice. These include cultural factors, such as the mission or vision of the school. For example, a public, magnet program or a parochial school will set a different

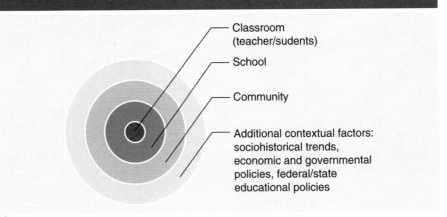

Figure 1.1   Nested Layers of Education Ecology

Classroom
(teacher/sudents)

School

Community

Additional contextual factors:
sociohistorical trends,
economic and governmental
policies, federal/state
educational policies

*factors that
impact school*

tone regarding the scope and direction of academic activities. Personnel factors, including the effectiveness of school leadership teams and the talent and training of teachers and staff in the building, will similarly impact the school climate. Curriculum and instructional guidance and support, resources and materials, and building facilities all impact the day-to-day practice of teachers and students.

Schools, of course, are institutions situated within local communities, often reflecting the relative level of wealth or lack of resources of those communities. Geographic and regional factors as well as urban, rural, or suburban locations may also impact school resources. Schools reflect the demographics of local communities, and they are fundamentally impacted by local policies that determine the availability of infrastructure and resources. For example, schools in communities that lack quality health resources will serve students who may be dealing with health issues or crises. At the same time, schools situated in high-wealth districts tend to have stronger parent–teacher associations to supplement district funding. Local communities are the decades-long products of larger sociohistorical trends as well as economic and political policies. More specific to the educational context, federal and state educational policies, including testing programs, curriculum standards, and textbook adoption (to name a few), delimit curriculum and instruction in classrooms.

Action research problems can originate at any of the layers of the educational system described here—classroom, school, and community. Once you begin your action research study and delve more deeply into issues related to practice, you may find that issues related to practice can straddle multiple layers of the educational system. Mary discovered this as she pursued her action research in her fourth-grade classroom.

Policy and Practices Related to Homeless Children

Mary, a beginning fourth-grade teacher at an elementary school located in a small city, was in the middle of her action research project focused on developing strategies to motivate students to learn when she noticed that several of her students were checking out early at 3:00 p.m., although school was not dismissed until 3:30 p.m. Since she was a new teacher she was reluctant to ask questions. Instead, she admonished her students about the importance of staying for the full day and even considered assigning extra homework to those who left early. She felt that motivation and engagement could be greatly improved if her students stayed until the final bell. As part of her action research, Mary set aside time each morning during individual seat work to interview her students about their views of school and what motivates them to learn. During one of these interviews, a student somewhat reluctantly explained that she left school early to check into the nearby homeless shelter with her family. Upon further investigation, Mary discovered that the homeless shelter admitted clients for the night beginning at 3:00 p.m. During the winter months beds filled up quickly, so parents were taking their kids out of school early to ensure they would have a safe place to stay for the night.

Mary's experience provides just one example of the ways that organizations within one community, both with similar goals, may fail to communicate. In this case, both the school and the homeless shelter provided public services to vulnerable populations. Yet leaders in both organizations failed to consider the broader systems in which they operated. The shelter was unwittingly disrupting the education of children whose families relied on the shelter. Mary little knew, nor understood, the conditions in which her children were living. No amount of goading or punishment could overcome her students' need for safety and shelter. Her action research challenged many of her preconceived notions and led her to work with her students in new ways, as well as to advocate for them.

Systems Theory

Systems theory (von Bertalanffy, 1968) and systems thinking have long been fundamental concepts in educational reform and instructional design. Proponents argue for a recognition of the interdependence and interconnectedness of educational systems; if one part of the system is changed, it alters the rest of the system (see Capra, 1982). Applied here to action research, systems thinking promotes the inclusion of all stakeholders in the design of effective educational systems and the recognition that stakeholder participation is necessary to bring about change within educational systems. "Stakeholder engagement is essential to the success of the design, adoption, and implementation of broad innovations such as new educational systems" (A. A. Carr, 1997, p. 6).

Returning to Figure 1.1, *stakeholders* refer to participants in each level of the educational system including teachers, students, school leaders, and community members. For those seeking change and improvement, approaches that are *systemic*—"holistic, contextualized and stakeholder-owned"—are preferred over systematic approaches that are "linear, generalizable, and typically top-down or expert driven" (A. A. Carr, 1997, p. 7). By engaging stakeholders who represent multiple perspectives and positions within educational systems, systemic change may occur. According to Carr (1997), "systemic change is broad in scope and large in scale. It entertains the whole system as a context for understanding change and organizational learning" (p. 9). While systems thinking takes into account the big picture, change is still largely dependent on the active participation of individuals. Since changes in one aspect of the system leads to changes in other areas, "systemic change recognizes the importance of user participation and responsibility within an organization that seeks change and improvement" (A. A. Carr, 1997, p. 9).

Perhaps systemic change in educational reform has been so difficult to achieve in the past because of a failure to actively engage individuals at all levels of the educational system. Much contemporary reform "pushes out" initiatives from a top-down perspective, ignoring the local and the contextual knowledge of individuals. Educational reformers seem to ignore teachers, imposing curriculum and instructional changes without engaging those charged with implementing change. Action research approaches educational change from a different direction—from the inside-out—and emphasizes personal interests and self-efficacy. Action research provides an approach to research that may engage whole communities and individual stakeholders in creating systemic change (Park, Brydon-Miller, Hall, & Jackson, 1993).

Rationale for Action Research

With such complex education systems in place, it is often difficult to tease out one or two particular factors that might improve classroom instruction and student outcomes. What action researchers understand is that there is much work to be done to better understand the nuance of each aspect of the educational system, even as we work for change.

Action research can be used to examine the complexity of schools and classrooms and enable all stakeholders to make more informed decisions about how to bring about change that will benefit students. Referring back to Figure 1.1, we might envision action research taking part at any of the levels of the educational system or across the levels. For example, within the classroom, the teacher might conduct teacher action research by studying issues associated with everyday practice and becoming a student of her students. According to Lytle and

bring concerns to stakeholders to make change.

Cochran-Smith (1994), "what distinguishes more productive from less productive teachers may not be mastery of a knowledge base, but rather standing in a different relationship to one's own knowledge, to one's students as knowers, and to knowledge generation in the field" (p. 31). Individual teacher researchers might join together to conduct school-wide action research about topics relevant to larger issues facing the school. (See, for example, Painter's 2004 description of teacher research projects at Deer Park School.) And, of course, teachers and schools are not limited to their own building; they may reach out to engage community members in action research projects and/or across schools. By reporting their findings to policy makers at the local, state, and national levels, action researchers have an opportunity to shift the educational ecology. Action researchers refine and share their **craft knowledge** through reflection in action. This work has profound import for both the individual practitioner-researcher and the educational community as a whole.

Defining Action Research

There are various forms and affiliated approaches to action research, including teacher research, participatory action research, self-study, and practitioner research. "Practitioner research" is often used as an umbrella term to describe approaches to research focused directly on issues related to practice. For example, Borko, Whitcomb, and Byrnes (2008) also describe "action research," "participatory research," "self-study," and "teacher research" as distinct genres of "practitioner research" (p. 1029; see also Rearick & Feldman, 1999, for a description of various distinctions across these types of practitioner research).

This text will refer to action research as "systematic and intentional inquiry" into practice (Cochran-Smith & Lytle, 1993, p. 7). Action research goes beyond casual observation or reflection to follow a formal structure of inquiry. Action researchers identify issues of deep importance relevant to practice, collect and analyze data, and share their findings. By formalizing the process of inquiry, the structure of action research creates a space for practitioners to pursue issues of real importance and to engage stakeholders through their data collection and analysis.

Due to the range of approaches and outcomes, there has been considerable discussion within the research literature about the relative merits of practical and more critical forms of action research. Practical action research studies may focus on teaching strategies and issues of practical interest or everyday relevance. Critical action research goes deeper toward the study of social, cultural, and political contexts of schooling in the pursuit of more just and democratic schools and society (e.g., W. Carr & Kemmis, 1986; Elliott, 1985; Hyland & Noffke, 2005; Kincheloe, 1991, 1995). Table 1.1 provides an overview of the differences between practical and critical action research.

Table 1.1 A Summary: Practical Action Research Compared to Critical Action Research

Practical Action Research	Critical Action Research
• "Practical-Deliberative" (McKernan, 1996)	• "Critical-Emancipatory" (McKernan, 1996)
• Concerned with practical knowledge or craft knowledge	• Concerned with social and cultural factors that impact school
• Interest in day-to-day issues of practice	• Interest in democratic participation and emancipation
• May result in improved practice and student performance but not social or cultural change	• Seeks deep change and enlightenment within the classroom
	• Implicit goal toward improving society

Source: Adapted from Manfra (2009).

Practical Inquiry

According to Cochran-Smith and Lytle (1999), action research theorized as practical inquiry is a "way to generate or enhance practical knowledge" (p. 19). They contend that "theorizers in this [practical] group assume that some of the most essential knowledge for teaching is practical knowledge" (p. 19). Here action research becomes a tool toward improving teaching and learning. For example, by focusing on specific pedagogical strategies and other topics that impact daily practice, the action researcher may focus on ways to improve the day-to-day outcomes of classroom practice. According to Cochran-Smith and Lytle, "practical inquiry is more likely to respond to the immediacy of the knowledge needs teachers confront in everyday practice and to be foundational for formal research by providing new questions and concerns" (p. 19). Practical action research can address concerns related to curriculum and instruction, as well as logistical issues related to planning and implementing teaching.

Perhaps due to the close coupling with everyday practice, practical action research is viewed as being more relevant and authentic for teachers. According to Glanz (1999),

> [practical] action research is a kind of research that has reemerged as a popular way of helping practitioners, teachers, and supervisors to better understand their work. In action research, we apply traditional research approaches (e.g., ethnographic, descriptive, quasi-experimental, and so forth) to real problems or issues faced by the practitioner. (p. 301)

The emphasis here is on practical, everyday problems that hinder effective practice.

Critical Inquiry

Proponents of critical forms of action research go beyond issues related to daily practice, to emphasize action research for real social change and the development of a more just and democratic society (e.g., Elliott, 1985; Gitlin & Haddon, 1997; Gore & Zeichner, 1991; Hyland & Noffke, 2005; Kemmis & Grundy, 1997; Kincheloe, 1991; Noffke, 1997; Van Manen, 1990). According to Kincheloe (1995), "the critical teacher researcher asks questions of deep structure of his or her school or classroom settings—in other words, he or she takes Habermas's (1972) notion of emancipatory interest of knowledge seriously" (p. 81). Here the action researcher is able to conceive of individual classrooms or practice as situated within complex sociocultural and political systems.

The aim of critical action research is not only to bring about change in one facet of the system but to eventually transform the whole. According to Cochran-Smith and Lytle (1999), "the emphasis is on transforming educational theory and practice toward emancipatory ends and thus raising fundamental questions about curriculum, teachers' roles, and the ends as well as the means of schooling" (p. 18). Proponents of critical action research are often critical of more "benign" forms of practical action research. According to Johnston (2005),

> On this [critical] view, we are encouraged to critique the social norms and practices that underlie our teaching practices and that may obstruct schooling for social justice. From this point of view, it is not enough to examine only teaching practice; teachers must also consider social and political influences on the teacher and students, as well as on schooling more generally. (pp. 65–66)

 The aim for critical action research is to work toward social justice and to interrogate the contexts of practice.

Middle Ground

The relevant literature regarding practical and critical action research appears to polarize the two camps. Yet the realities of practice and the work of individuals within educational systems cannot be so neatly divided into practical and critical concerns. In creating a dichotomy between practical and critical action research, theorizers seem to have needlessly created opposing camps. Practitioners understand that the day-to-day issues of practice cannot be separated from the complex contexts of educational systems. Exploring the seemingly mundane may reveal critical sociocultural issues. Often both practical and critical concerns are interwoven across the classroom, school, and community contexts.

This text will focus on a middle ground whereby practical action research studies can lead to critical outcomes for teachers, students, schools, and communities. Envisioning a middle ground provides space for teachers and other practitioners to negotiate the tensions, practical concerns, and critical issues they face in their daily practice. Regardless of the scope of the issues confronted, action researchers follow a cycle that includes the same systematic steps.

Main Features of Action Research

The main features of the **action research cycle** tend to parallel the inquiry cycle followed in educational and ethnographic social science research—posing questions and collecting and analyzing data to answer those questions. One major difference exists, however: Action research follows a cycle of inquiry in which each iteration builds on the previous and leads to the next. Also, unlike positivist or postpositivist versions of scientific research, conclusions are co-constructed with research participants (often students or other teachers) and findings are more context-specific and tentative. This approach to research honors the professional knowledge or craft knowledge of the researcher while also acknowledging subjectivity and positionality in educational research.

Over the course of this book, we will explore the major parts of the action research cycle:

- Problem posing (posing research questions, reviewing literature)

- Action (planning and initiating the study)

- Observation (collecting data)

- Reflection (analyzing data and writing final reports)

- Sharing (disseminating findings and developing an action plan)

These steps should be viewed as part of a cycle, as in Figure 1.2.

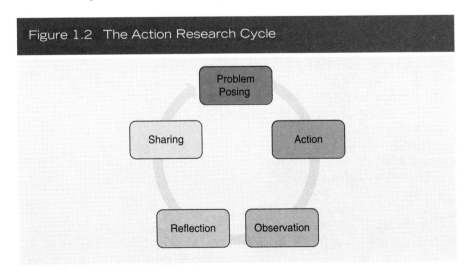

Figure 1.2 The Action Research Cycle

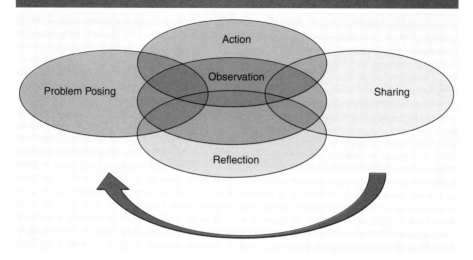

Figure 1.3 Action Research as an Iterative Cycle

Action

Observation

Problem Posing

Sharing

Reflection

However, although the steps will be described in separate chapters, they should be viewed as overlapping and iterative. Figure 1.3 demonstrates how these steps overlap and inform each other; for example, observation is a part of action, and analysis and reflection are ongoing.

Change as the Desired Outcome

Regardless of the scope or topic under investigation, action research is not a static approach to conducting educational research. Whereas traditional approaches to research focus on expert knowledge, here the role of the researcher is facilitative and self-reflective. The overall aim is to bring about change through the research process. According to Johnston (2005), "taking action and studying its consequences for student learning is the hallmark of action research. The action is intended to create change for the better and the study is intended to find out if it does" (p. 60). This change may include changing "craft knowledge," changing educational practices, and changing the culture of schooling. By its very nature, action research is defined by change.

Action Research and Craft Knowledge

Craft knowledge refers to the tacit knowledge or implicit insights a teacher holds about practice; it guides daily practice and teachers come to rely on it to make decisions in the classroom. Action research provides a systematic and intentional approach for practitioners to reflect on and improve their craft knowledge.

According to Grimmett and MacKinnon (1992), "craft knowledge consists of pedagogical content and pedagogical learner knowledge derived from considered experience in the practice setting" (p. 387). Thus, they combine Shulman's (1987) pedagogical content knowledge—"[the] special amalgam of content and pedagogy" (p. 8)—with pedagogical learner knowledge—"the procedural ways in which teachers deal rigorously and supportively with learners" (Grimmett & MacKinnon, 1992, p. 387). Craft knowledge refers to the judgment teachers exercise as well as the "'glue' that brings all of the knowledge bases to bear on the act of teaching" (p. 387). It is the contextualized knowledge that experienced, skilled practitioners possess through the "wisdom of practice" (Shulman, 1987). Craft knowledge guides the daily curricular and pedagogical decisions that teachers make—it is the "know-how" that practitioners rely on regularly and can be "a powerful determinant of teachers' practice" (p. 388). At the same time, it has its limits. Craft knowledge fails if it "do[es] not improve practice from the learners' perspective" (p. 388) or if it does not take into account changing contexts.

Action research provides a structure for practitioners to study, interrogate, and reflect on their craft knowledge. By making implicit understanding explicit, teachers reveal their insider knowledge. By taking an inquiry stance toward this knowledge base, they can systematically and intentionally study their assumptions. As a result, teachers can make more reasoned decisions about their practices and work toward improvement. Teachers may also find evidence to support the efficacy of their craft knowledge. Falk and Blumenreich (2005) explain, "an unanticipated, but pleasant outcome for teachers who have engaged in research about their own questions has been finding affirmation for ideas and practices that were previously intuitive" (p. 177). By making intuitive knowledge more explicit, action researchers make sense of their work.

The action research process may also challenge previously held beliefs. Through the action research process, teachers may extend, refine, and improve their pedagogical content knowledge. An important part of this process is for action researchers to share their findings. By sharing their craft knowledge through action research reports, conference presentations, or more informal avenues, teachers can provide insights with "profound implications for the education of practitioners" (Grimmett & MacKinnon, 1992, p. 388) and the educational community in general.

Reflection in Action

Reflection is an important element of action research and has been shown to contribute to the development and refinement of craft knowledge. Teaching practice especially is developed and improved through reflective practice. "Teaching should be viewed as a craft that includes a reflective approach toward problems, a cultivation of imagination, and a playfulness toward words, relationships, and experiences" (Tom, 1984, p. 113). This reflective approach goes beyond the casual reflection most teachers engage in on a daily basis to include a more systematic and intentional approach to **reflection in action**. Schön (1983) referred to "reflection-in-action" and "reflection-on-action" as two interrelated approaches to changing practice through systematic reflection. The assumption is that reflection about practice both during practice and before and after will necessarily impact the practice under study.

The emphasis on reflection in action research has also been traced to the work of John Dewey (1933), who emphasized that the process of reflective inquiry must become "persistent" in education. Action research provides a framework for ongoing or persistent reflection. According to Cochran Smith and Lytle (1993), "Dewey emphasized the importance of teachers' reflecting on their practices and integrating their observations into their emerging theories of teaching and learning" (p. 9). This approach to defining and refining knowledge about practice is fundamental to action researchers. Reflection is an important part of the cycle because it leads to new questions and sparks further inquiry.

Rigorous reflection leads to changes in practice. According to Price (2001), reflection and inquiry can help teachers and teacher candidates "develop their 'habits of mind,' through looking retrospectively on the teaching that has occurred, reconstructing, re-enacting, and recapturing events, and critically analysing their students' and their own actions, with explanations supported with evidence" (p. 48). Critical analysis or reflection leads to new habits of mind or professional knowledge. This work is complex and includes focusing on aspects of practice across the educational ecology. According to Price, "this [reflection] involves, for example, using knowledge to understand oneself, the complexity, uncertainty, and risky nature of teaching, the political and social dimensions of teaching and learning processes, and the consequences for children" (pp. 48–49). Ultimately, through reflective practice, teachers gain greater awareness of their impact on student learning and can adjust their teaching accordingly. Rogers, Noblit, and Ferrell (1990) note, "action research is a vehicle to put teachers in charge of their craft and its improvement" (p. 179). Here, teacher decision-making is informed by systematic and intentional inquiry into practice. In the process, teachers formalize their craft knowledge and work as professional decision makers.

Academic and Community Development

The benefits of conducting action research have been well documented in the relevant research literature. Beyond making craft knowledge more explicit and improving practice through systematic reflection, Falk and Blumenreich (2005) detail the positive outcomes for teachers engaging in teacher action research, including developing self-efficacy and becoming part of the professional community or feeling more like a profession. This is because, by making craft knowledge more explicit and generating theories of practice through the action research process, teachers find themselves in new positions within the educational system. According to Lytle and Cochran-Smith (1994), "if we regard teachers' theories as sets of interrelated conceptual frameworks grounded in practice, then teacher researchers are revealed as both users and generators of theory" (p. 28). The notion of practitioners as generators of theory, not just consumers who enact theory, alters the traditional top-down approach of most school reform. As action researchers, practitioners are empowered to share their knowledge, to influence the practice of others, and to provide leadership within the educational system.

In the next chapter, we will explore strategies for posing questions about issues of deep importance that can spark an action research study. We will examine ways that action researchers develop questions by exploring issues of practice at various levels of the educational system. By identifying topics that are both professionally and personally important, practitioners can discern how their experiences fit within the larger frame of the educational system. By working with co-researchers and sharing findings from their action research, practitioners at all levels make their craft knowledge more explicit and provide new ideas about ways to bring about change.

CHAPTER SUMMARY

- Action research provides a more personal and nuanced approach to addressing contemporary educational reform issues.

- Action research flips the typical top-down approaches to educational reform and engages practitioners as problem solvers.

- Action research can be used to solve issues across the educational system.

- Systems thinking or systems theory points to the interdependence and interconnectedness of educational reform issues.

- Action research can be used to examine the complexity of schools and classrooms

and enable all stakeholders to make more informed decisions about how to bring about change that will benefit students.

- Action research refers to the systematic and intentional approach to studying issues related to practice.

- The action research cycle follows a series of steps, including problem posing, action observation, reflection, and sharing.

- Through reflection in action and reflection on action, action researchers engage in the study and implementation of changing practice.

SUGGESTED WEB-BASED RESOURCES

Understanding Action Research (Center for Collaborative Action Research)

http://cadres.pepperdine.edu/ccar/define.html

Action Research (BBC)

https://www.teachingenglish.org.uk/article/action-research

Action Research

https://www.brown.edu/academics/education-alliance/sites/brown.edu.academics.education-alliance/files/publications/act_research.pdf

QUESTIONS AND ACTIVITIES

Reflection Questions

1. In your own words, how do you define action research?

2. What role might action research play in contemporary educational reform?

3. What are research topics that might originate at each of the layers of the educational system described here? (e.g., classroom, school, and community level)

4. How can action research improve practice?

5. What are differences between practical and critical action research?

6. What are differences between action research and other forms of educational research?

Practice Activities

Activity 1A: Understanding Action Research Through Inductive Analysis

Action researchers often use inductive approaches to analyzing data. This activity will engage students in inductively analyzing action research reports, while also engaging them in developing their own definitions of action research.

Select three action research studies to read. Suggested examples include the following:

Ballenger, C. (1996). Learning the ABCs in a Haitian preschool: A teacher's story. *Language Arts, 73,* 317–323.

Bouillion, L. M., & Gomez, L. M. (2001). Connecting school and community with science learning: Real world problems and school–community partnerships as contextual scaffolds. *Journal of Research in Science Teaching, 38,* 878–898.

Burns, T. J. (2009). Searching for peace: Exploring issues of war with young children. *Language Arts, 86,* 421–430.

Catapano, S., & Song, K. H. (2006). Let's collaborate and infuse citizenship education: Kids voting in primary classrooms. *Social Studies Research and Practice, 1*(1), 55–66.

Fecho, B. (2001). "Why are you doing this?" Acknowledging and transcending threat in a critical inquiry classroom. *Research in the Teaching of English, 36*(1), 9–37.

Hackenberg, A. J. (2010). Mathematical caring relations in action. *Journal for Research in Mathematics Education, 41,* 236–273.

Hyland, N. E., & Noffke, S. E. (2005). Understanding diversity through social and community inquiry: An action research study. *Journal of Teacher Education, 56,* 367–381.

James, J. H. (2008). Teachers as protectors: Making sense of preservice teachers' resistance to interpretation in elementary history teaching. *Theory & Research in Social Education, 36,* 172–205.

Kelley, L. (2006). Learning to question in kindergarten. *Social Studies Research and Practice, 1*(1), 45–54.

Levin, B. B, & Rock, T. C. (2003). The effects of collaborative action research on preservice and experienced teacher partners in professional development schools. *Journal of Teacher Education, 54,* 135–149.

Martell, C. C. (2015). Learning to teach culturally relevant social studies: A White teacher's retrospective self-study. In P. Chandler (Ed.), *Doing race in social studies: Critical perspectives* (pp. 41–60). New York, NY: Information Age.

Wade, R. C. (1999). Voice and choice in a university seminar: The struggle to teach democratically. *Theory & Research in Social Education, 27,* 70–92.

Also, see examples reprinted in: MacLean, M. S., & Mohr, M. M. (1999). *Teacher-researchers at work.* Berkley, CA: National Writing Project.

Compare and contrast across the readings. Note key features of each study, including the approach to research, the interests of the researcher, and the outcomes. Ultimately, respond in writing to the following prompt: "Based on these readings, how would you define teacher research? What seem to be common characteristics across the studies?"

Activity 1B: Exploring Action Research Interests

Write a brief (one-page) explanation of an aspect of your practice that you would like to study more deeply. (This might form the basis for your project proposal that you will submit at the end of the semester.) Describe your research questions and offer a rationale for the significance/importance of the topic for study. Locate two or three articles related to the topic(s) you are interested in studying. Create brief annotations for each article.

Activity 1C: Understanding Your Worldview and Positionality

Unlike positivist or postpositivist forms of research, action researchers acknowledge their worldview and positionality. They understand that their experiences and perspectives will guide the choice of research questions they pursue and the manner in which they pursue them. By being clear about one's position, action researchers can develop more authentic accounts of their experiences. In this activity you will answer a series of questions to help you clarify your position.

Answer the following questions in as much detail as possible:

What is the purpose of schooling?

What knowledge is of most worth?

What should school teach?

What should be the role of the teacher in the classroom?

What should be the role of the student in the classroom?

What should be the relationship between the school and the community?

If you are a member of a class or research collaborative, you may wish to share your answers after answering these questions. You may also return to these questions from time to time over the course of your action research project to monitor how your own research may change or clarify your thinking on each item.

Guiding Questions

1. What are issues related to practice that come to mind as you reflect on your work?
2. Who might support your action research project or collaborate with you?
3. How might your worldview and experiences impact your action research?

Keywords and Glossary

Critical friends: provide feedback to action researchers about their work through each stage of the research process.

Gap analysis: is used to determine areas in need of further study; the difference between the desired and actual situation.

Interpretivist inquiry: emerges from a worldview that acknowledges the context-dependent nature of human experience and the importance of working alongside research participants to develop a more nuanced understanding of their experiences while also acknowledging the positionality of the researcher.

Needs assessment: is a systematic approach to understanding the status quo, by identifying what is and what ought to be.

Nominal group technique: provides a structure for gathering ideas from members of a collaborative group in the initial phases of a needs assessment or other form of collaborative inquiry project.

Positivist inquiry: emerges from a worldview in which knowledge claims and theories are derived through experimental or quasi-experimental means usually through a deductive approach to analyzing quantitative data.

"Something That Matters"

Action research might be undertaken by individual teachers or groups of teachers, across schools, or with community members. For each of these approaches, below are example action research projects, each situated within the nested layers of the complex educational system described in Chapter 1. Chapters later in the book will go into more detail about many of the methodological topics mentioned here.

This chapter serves as a starting point for reflecting upon and identifying potential research questions related to practice. Here we will explore various approaches to conducting educational research and develop a deeper understanding of purposes of action research. The approach we take here presupposes a middle ground between practical and critical forms of action research. The overall aim is to identify an issue that impacts daily practice while also working to bring about real change. Action researchers should begin in thoughtful contemplation about daily practice as well as how their actions respond to and are affected by various educational stakeholders.

Approaches to Educational Research

Often when practitioners are confronted with the responsibility of conducting research it seems like an overwhelming endeavor. This may be due in part to commonly held assumptions about research as controlled experiments. When research is seen as only being done by an objective outsider under controlled, lab-like conditions, it can feel impossible to integrate into daily practice. That approach to research originates from a **positivist inquiry** view of research in which knowledge claims or theories are derived through deductive means and most often through the collection of quantitative data.

However, there has been growing recognition within the educational research community that this positivist approach to defining research is too narrow. It does not take into account the importance of context and ignores insider knowledge. Proponents of action research and other forms of **interpretivist inquiry** have expanded the understanding of what "counts" as research to include more contextual, narrative, and critical approaches.

Teacher-conducted classroom-based inquiry has not always enjoyed such a prominent place in educational research. However, over the last decades, action research has been increasingly embraced by members of the American educational research community (Lagemann, 2000). This may be due in part to a growing interest in qualitative research methods and community-based and culturally relevant educational practices. It also aligns with contemporary understanding about the contextualized nature of educational research and the importance of working alongside participants to gain a more trustworthy understanding of their experiences. Willig (2014) explains the degree of appropriation that takes place during research and the consequences:

To interpret another person's experience means claiming to have access to (some of) its underlying meaning. During the act of interpretation the interpreter moves beyond the surface meaning of a description or representation and asks: "What does it mean?" As a result, the act of interpretation always involves a degree of appropriation; the interpreter processes what he or she sees, hears and/or reads, digests it, metabolizes it and generates something new. (p. 11)

Since interpretation is such an important component of educational research, it is essential that university-based researchers engage participants, especially practitioners in research endeavors. Action research provides a framework for engaging practitioners in interpreting their own practice.

The subjective nature of educational research requires that researchers clarify their beliefs, views, and values. By reflecting on what matters most, action researchers become clearer about their education philosophies or worldviews. All of which has implications for future directions of the research since "people tend to adhere to the methodology that is most consonant with their socialized worldview" (Glesne, 1999, p. 8). For example, Egbert and Sanden (2014) suggest a tree metaphor in which epistemology serves as the roots of a research project and the conceptual framework is the ground from which the tree grows.

Many have argued that the very nature of action research—engaging practitioners and other stakeholders actively in the research endeavor—necessitates approaching research from an interpretivist conceptual framework. According to Schwandt (1989),

Our constructions of the world, our values, our ideas about how to inquire into those constructions, are mutually self-reinforcing. We conduct inquiry via a particular paradigm because it embodies assumptions about the world that we believe and values that we hold, and because we hold those assumptions and values we conduct inquiry according to the precepts of that paradigm. (p. 399)

In this sense then, action research aligns with a particular paradigm—one that values multiple perspectives, the contextualized nature of experience and knowledge, and the willingness to empower voices that have been traditionally marginalized.

For example, a teacher interested in engaging in action research is turning the tables on traditional power relationships in the classroom by providing voice to students and becoming a "student" of her students. According to Glesne (1999), "In recent years, increased sensitivity to issues of power and authority has encouraged a rethinking of research design and implementation" (p. 9). Whereas some believe that the "authority for research decisions resides with the researcher" (p. 9), action researchers challenge this notion. "In particular, they [action researchers] cause us to rethink the purpose of research and, thereby, researcher-researched partnerships" (p. 9). An important starting point for action research is to reflect on your positionality and to identify issues that might be addressed through systematic and intentional inquiry about practice.

Identifying an Action Research Topic: Problem Posing and Reflection

In action research, the practitioner becomes the meaning-maker, generating new knowledge or theory through the systematic and intentional investigation of issues related to practice. As such, action research projects originate from issues of real importance for practitioners. They often emerge in the gap between the desired outcomes and the realities of day-to-day practice. Action research projects might also emerge from special circumstances—for example, issues raised in contemporary teacher evaluation practices including value-added assessments, edTPA, and National Board certification (see the special section dedicated to these issues below) or through graduate education and other extended professional development opportunities.

An important first step toward identifying an action research topic and posing a problem to study is to engage in observation and reflection. Observation may include the collection of data as well as more informal information gathering, for example, discussing ideas with colleagues or other stakeholders. It is also important during this stage to review relevant literature and to reflect on issues raised through conversation or in writing in a researcher journal. (See Activity 2A for suggested prompts to guide your thinking, writing, and reflection.)

Gap Analysis and Problem Posing in Action Research

Another strategy for developing an action research project is to conduct a gap analysis—exploring the difference between what is and what ought to be. In order to understand the "gap" between the desired outcomes and the actual outcomes or status quo, researchers gather data about what is actually happening and compare this to the desired outcome. By identifying the gap, the action researcher identifies an important area in need of attention and further study. An action research project might then go on to determine why the gap exists and how to bring about change to correct it. (See Activity 2B for an example Gap Analysis Worksheet.)

Action Research Case Studies and Understanding Your Impact on Student Learning

Arlene's action research study emerged from her interest in learning how to better impact student learning. Student learning is an issue of deep concern for stakeholders at all levels of the educational system and an ethical imperative for teachers and administrators. Meta-analysis studies of action research have demonstrated

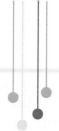

Vignette: Arlene's Action Research

Creating a More Culturally Relevant Middle School Classroom

Arlene was concerned that the African American male students in her seventh-grade classroom were underperforming on classroom-based assessments. Her gap analysis was fairly simple and straightforward: She compared assessment data between her African American students and their classmates and noted a disturbing pattern. Whereas her desired outcome would be for all of her students to be achieving fairly consistently, in practice, student assessment scores ranged widely. She also noted marked differences in behavior and motivation during her teaching—her African American students seemed disengaged and frustrated. Arlene reflected on the initial data she gathered as well as her own experiences teaching. She sought out literature to help her understand what other educators had discovered about the achievement gap and ways to address it in the classroom.

that action researchers can positively impact student learning when they systematically and intentionally focus on student achievement.

Perhaps one benefit of contemporary educational reform is the persistent focus on improving student learning outcomes. Many states and districts have developed teacher evaluation programs that include measures related to student learning. Preservice teachers at most accredited institutions are expected to provide evidence of their impact on student learning as part of edTPA (formerly the Teacher Performance Assessment; edtpa.aacte.org) and experienced teachers must do the same to achieve National Board Certification (www.nbpts.org). These outcome-based assessments go beyond previous approaches of teacher assessment to include data about actual student performance.

Although current measures of teacher effectiveness include a focus on student learning outcomes on standardized tests, teachers still have latitude in determining how to measure their effectiveness. In fact, it seems crucial that teachers include qualitative data to help explain and provide more nuance to test score data. For example, on a recent survey conducted by *Education Week* (2016) teachers overwhelmingly agreed that motivation and engagement are two of the most important factors in student achievement. At the same time, "more than half of the teachers (51%) said it is a challenge to reach struggling, apathetic, or resistant students" (n.p.). If the perceived link between student achievement and student motivation is so strong, its follows that teachers must better understand not only the level of achievement in their classroom but also the level of student motivation. Stated another way, any study about improving achievement must also connect with research about how to motivate and engage students.

Standardized test scores could become one part of a more complex effort to understand a teacher's impact on student learning. By becoming "students" of their students, action researchers learn about not only what their students know but why they know it and how they came to know. Perhaps most importantly, they also begin to understand how they, as teachers, have contributed to student learning. Getting a good sense of student achievement at the beginning of an action research project, through a gap analysis or some other method, provides practitioners with an important baseline on which to build future work.

Given what we know about the complexity of educational systems, it is not surprising that action research projects that embark on a study of student learning often lead to directions not previously considered by the action researcher. These might include issues related to learning contexts, curriculum materials, instructional strategies, student factors, and assessment strategies. There are numerous additional text and web-based resources for understanding your impact on student learning (see resources listed at the end of the chapter).

Collaborative Action Research Projects

Understanding issues related to practice, particularly student learning outcomes, is a complex process and it may be beneficial for action researchers to engage in collaborative action research projects with peers and colleagues. It may even be possible for collaborative action research groups to leverage preexisting organizational structures within schools and communities to support their work. For example, many schools use a departmental structure to organize teachers by grade level or subject areas in professional learning teams (PLTs) or communities (PLCs).

Endeavoring an action research project as a department or PLT provides an organizing framework within which individuals might work. Here, research groups are usually composed of about three to five teachers and may meet every two to three weeks throughout the school year (MacLean & Mohr, 1999). Within these groups, teachers can develop working relationships to support each other during each stage in the process of action research. For instance, research group members might refine research topics and data collection methods through deliberation and conversation. In addition to providing support, research group members might challenge each other's assumptions, provide feedback on written drafts of reports of findings, and propose alternative ideas or interpretations. Cornelissen, vanSwet, Beijaard, and Bergen (2011) explain that the "relationships in the research partnership can be collaborative with a high degree of mutual engagement; the research agendas, methods and outcomes are negotiated and collective research activities are undertaken" (p. 148). Effective research partnerships provide ongoing support while also enabling researchers to pursue individual lines of inquiry. Within collaborative action research groups, individual members are free to both explore issues of personal concern and contribute to the group's investigation. For action research projects that engage more than one researcher, the members of the group may also decide to conduct a needs assessment—a strategy for more systematically understanding the current situation and posing problems to address over the course of the action research.

Needs Assessment

Needs assessment is a common feature of program evaluation. Often used by schools, it can be adapted to larger- or smaller-scale action research projects. To get started, a common technique for conducting a needs assessment is to follow the "gap model" (e.g., Kaufman & English, 1979). The model includes three phases: "1. goal setting, identifying what ought to be; 2. performance measurement, determining what is; 3. discrepancy identification, ordering differences between what ought to be and what it is" (McKillip, 1987, p. 20). The needs assessment will provide an understanding of a baseline or starting point, which is invaluable for action researchers intent on bringing about change. This systematic approach to understanding the status quo not only helps the researcher identify *what is*, but it also brings into focus *what ought to be*.

In order to begin the goal-setting stage of a needs assessment, you can follow a **nominal group technique** (Moore, 1987). This approach is often helpful in early stages of needs assessments in which you plan to engage multiple stakeholders. According to Moore (1987), "the [nominal group] technique is helpful in identifying problems, exploring solutions, and establishing priorities" (p. 10). Most importantly, this technique provides an opportunity for everyone to share their input and ensure diversity of ideas.

In the nominal group technique, the facilitator begins by outlining an issue or topic. Each member of the group is given a set amount of time to silently brainstorm ideas and jot down as many as possible. Once the time is up, each member of the group reports one idea. At this stage, there is no group discussion. Rather, the facilitator simply records each idea, going around to each member of the group until all of the ideas have been recorded. Next, each idea is discussed as a group. Individual ideas can be combined, altered, or deleted based on the consensus of the group. Finally, the group prioritizes the list to determine the most important items for the group to pursue. The vignette below demonstrates how the nominal group technique was used to guide a needs assessment conducted in a large school district.

Professional Learning Communities

Many schools and districts in the United States have already adopted a collaborative culture through the formation of PLCs (DuFour & Eaker, 1998) and PLTs. These may also be leveraged for action research projects. Since inquiry and change are both hallmarks of PLCs and PLTs, it is likely that members of well-functioning groups will be able to pick up the research cycle and use it to more systematically study issues of importance. According to DuFour, DuFour, Eaker, and Many (2010), characteristics of "high-performing PLCs" include "collective inquiry" and "action orientation of 'learning by doing.'" Although they do not specifically mention action research methodology, it seems that it is a natural fit for the work of PLCs.

Action research provides a structure for organizing the work of PLCs. This work is most often successful in schools and districts where teachers are provided

Vignette: Needs Assessment of Social Studies Professional Development

When a group of educators in a public school system set out to determine the current state of teaching American history and ways to improve the curriculum, they began by developing a list of priorities. To do this they conducted a needs assessment with the goal of developing, providing, and evaluating professional development for American history teachers in the district. The rationale was that, by better understanding the gap between the current and desired experiences in these areas, the district could design a professional development program that would be responsive to the specific needs of local teachers, students, and administrators.

This action research was initiated not only to help plan future professional development programming but also to evaluate the effectiveness of current teaching practices. It began with a working group meeting that included the curriculum directors for secondary and elementary social studies as well as a representative from the school district's office of assessment and evaluation. When this group met they followed the nominal group technique (Moore, 1987) to structure the meeting and to facilitate discussion about history instruction and professional development in the county. As a group they began by individually responding in writing on a "Gap Analysis Worksheet" to explore the differences between the desired and actual experiences of teaching history and conducting professional development in the county. Next, they shared their responses and created a master list. Finally, they evaluated

assessment data from the previous years. Over the course of the discussion, one member of the group recorded key issues.

Data collected from the nominal group meeting provided the basis for the development of two surveys for American history teachers in the district. Following McKillip's advice (1987), "They [surveys] provide[d] a flexible means of assessing the expectations both of subgroups of the target population and of other audiences to the need analysis" (p. 60). The surveys included a series of closed and open-ended questions designed to gauge teacher experiences. The surveys were sent to middle and high school (Grades 6–12) social studies teachers and to elementary (Grades 3–5) teachers in the district using a free online survey tool. Both qualitative and quantitative data from the surveys were analyzed. Surveys were followed by focus group and individual interviews with 15 teachers from elementary, middle, and high schools in the county. The interviews were transcribed verbatim and coded using a constant comparative method.

Based on the data from the working group, teacher surveys, and follow-up interviews, the team of action researchers developed a tentative hypothesis and reconvened the working group to discuss findings, again using a nominal group technique. Based on the feedback from the group, they went on to revise their initial interpretations and developed a list of recommendations for the district. Based on these recommendations, a professional development plan was developed and initiated across the district.

"the conditions that support meaningful teamwork" (DuFour & Fullan, 2013, p. 67). These conditions include supporting the development of collaborative teams (either by grade level or subject area) and providing adequate time for curriculum development, planning, implementation, and analysis of student work. PLCs may provide the "space" within the school day to enable teachers and other school personnel to pursue action research projects.

Working With Critical Friends

Regardless of whether practitioners engage in action research as individuals or in collaborative groups, it is important to share with **critical friends** throughout the process. Critical friends provide the necessary support of probing for meaning and offering feedback about action research projects. As the name suggests, critical friends provide constructive criticism, meant in the best sense, to further the interests of the researcher. By engaging critical friends early in the process, action researchers can test out ideas and monitor their own understanding. As they move through each stage in the action research cycle, researchers can share initial findings and reflections. Critical friends can push for deeper reflection and meaning making. A critical friend can balance being a friend—"someone who will listen and is trusted enough by colleagues for them to take risks"—and being critical—"the relationship is sufficiently robust to cope with questions and differing viewpoints . . . confront[ing] issues that have the potential to be taken for granted or unnoticed by the school community" (Aubusson, Ewing, & Francis, 2009, p. 76). There is no doubt that action research can feel like a risky endeavor for those involved. By opening oneself to scrutiny and being willing to admit the need for change, action researchers acknowledge their fallibility. Critical friends can be there to support the action researcher throughout the process to ensure fidelity to the model as well as to provide an essential reality check.

Engaging With Web-Based Collaboratives

Web-based collaboratives can provide an additional source of support for action researchers as well as a venue for sharing research findings (Cochran-Smith & Lytle, 2009; McNiff & Whitehead, 2010). These collaboratives are especially invaluable for action researchers that do not have access to co-researchers or critical friends. According to Cochran-Smith and Lytle (2009), emerging technologies have "spawned innovative uses of technology for sharing inquiries and classroom practices with audiences" (p. 22). Web-based collaboratives may be subject-specific or open to action researchers from a variety of backgrounds. Examples include the Bread Loaf Network (see Lewis, Guerrero, Makikana, & Armstrong, 2002), the Carnegie Foundation's CASTL Program for K–12 teachers/teacher educators (see also Hatch, 2006; Hatch & Shulman, 2005), and the Collaborative Action Research Network (CARN). (See the list of web-based collaboratives at the end of the chapter.)

CARN is one of the oldest and most well-established collaborative networks for action researchers. Established in 1976 by John Elliott and a small group of teacher researchers with help from a grant from the Ford Foundation, it has grown over time to include members representing multiple disciplines and research interests. According to Somekh (2010), a long-time member and leader of CARN, the C stood for Classroom rather than Collaborative although "CARN has its roots specifically within the educative values inherent in the words 'teacher' and 'teaching'" (p. 104). In other words, the focus of the network from the beginning was to "provide a forum for making teachers' knowledge public as a sound basis for curriculum development" (p. 106) and, by extension, school reform. Over time, the CARN bulletins (1977–1991) and, beginning in 1993, the journal *Educational Action Research (EAR)* provided a forum for teachers and other practitioners to share their work.

"Today CARN is well established as an international network that supports action researchers in local contexts and strengthens the collaborative relations of the global action research community" (Somekh, 2010, p. 110). Perhaps most importantly, CARN encourages cross-cultural collaboration as well as collaboration among practitioners from a variety of backgrounds and experiences. Teachers and other educators can tap into the rich resources and opportunities to collaborate and share work through CARN's publications, conferences, and website.

Action Research Across the Educational System

As the work of CARN suggests, there is no reason for action research to be limited to practitioners with similar roles. Instead, much can be gained from action research projects that span multiple layers of the educational system. In such instances, each practitioner will bring important knowledge to bear on a pertinent educational issue. For example, teachers and administrators may work together to improve classroom management and discipline policies in a school. By also engaging members of the community including parents, church leaders, and community groups, they can begin to understand complex issues related to student behavior and collaboratively develop programs to bring about change within the school. It is recommended that collaborative teams establish common goals around issues related to practice. Team members will benefit from "shared responsibility for engaging in collective inquiry" (DuFour & Fullan, 2013) around issues of deep and immediate importance.

Action research also provides a strategy for rethinking the traditional "turnaround" models of school reform. Rather than initiate these models as top-down, outside-in approaches to "fixing" bad schools, action research can provide a systematic and intentional approach to empowering practitioners to improve schools from within. For schools that pursue this direction, a crucial first step is to collectively identify persistent and pressing issues.

After key issues are identified by the nominal group, members of the school community, with the help of its leadership team, can move on to break these issues down into smaller, more manageable projects. These projects can be assigned to various action research teams within a school or community, creating a distributed research environment that contributes to a common goal. As each smaller team of action researchers conducts their inquiry, it is essential to plan for periodic meetings in which teams share their interim case analysis, including data collection and findings, as well as to plan a final culminating end point for sharing findings and making plans for future work. A suggested timeline follows:

Summer I – Issue Framing

- Conduct needs assessment
- Initiate nominal group meetings to identify core issues
- Divide into smaller action research teams
- Clarify individual roles in the research endeavor, sort out logistical issues (time, access to data, etc.), and identify final work product (e.g., research report, presentation, policy brief)

Fall (October) – Midterm Interim Case Analysis

- Write up interim case analysis to share initial research findings
- Provide updates about current data collection efforts and (if necessary) refine research problems and reorganize teams
- Conduct an audit of resources (Do teams have the necessary time and support needed to carry out their work?)

January – Midyear Interim Case Analysis

- Provide update about data collection, analysis, and initial findings
- Plan for second half of action research study (if necessary), refine research problems, and reorganize teams
- Continue to audit resource and logistical issues

Spring (March or April) – Midterm Case Analysis

- Provide updates about data collection and analysis
- Share findings and initial directions for policy changes and future work
- Share drafts of final work product

Vignette: Community Group Approaches to Action Research

In Seattle, Mitchell and Elwood (2012) conducted a participatory action research project to engage seventh-grade girls in "*counter-mapping* to resist hegemonic ways of representing space" (italics in original, p. 158). The authors aimed toward "enhancing students' sense of their own knowledge and agency to impact their communities, and developing research outputs that foster sustainable benefits for their communities" (p. 143). More specifically, they sought to understand whether students investigating institutions associated with marginalized groups would guide the students toward greater understanding about long-term sociohistoric trends and strategies for becoming civically engaged. They were "interested in whether learning about these historical processes would seem more immediate and important to the students if they could visualize how and where these things occurred" (p. 158). During the project, the seventh graders mapped key historical sites in Seattle using the Google Maps API and created annotations (photos, comments, etc.). They also created think-alouds or "guided tours" of maps discussing what was included/excluded and why, as well as responded to a civic engagement worksheet. The adult participants (Mitchell and Elwood) kept field journals of their observations about youth participants as well as analyzed samples of students' work. As a result of their study, the authors concluded:

> Among the insights that the students derived, a key one was the growing understanding that both discriminatory actions such as redlining, and the creation of affirmative locales such as benevolent societies, are profoundly spatial processes critical in both scope and impact to historically subordinated groups. (p. 157)

This action research project was unique in engaging youth participants as co-researchers. The aim here was to study "a social situation with a view to improving the quality of action within it" (Elliott, 1991, p. 69). The collaborative action research followed a systematic approach or cycle that included problem posing, action, observation, reflection, and sharing. Through systematic and intentional inquiry and reflection, the participants in the project worked for change at various levels in the educational system.

Summer II – Summative Research Symposium

- Share final work products
- Initiate nominal groups to craft policy changes based on findings
- Develop action plans
- Initiate future action research and reform endeavors

The importance of professional development, collaboration, and trust cannot be overemphasized in such a model. It is essential for action researchers to feel their work connects with their day-to-day work and that they have the necessary time and support for these endeavors. By being very purposeful in the framing and organizing stages, school leaders can help guide individual action researchers through any apprehension that might exist and to help navigate the sticky points. Through careful planning, widespread commitment, and time, action research can provide a means to reframe educational institutions in a way that is more sustainable than having outside groups lead the work.

Educators and educational researchers can also develop action research projects that engage students as active participants in the meaning-making. Rarely given a voice in educational policy, students experience the day-to-day effects of educational and social policies. It seems desirable then to engage students in identifying issues of concern as well as in developing solutions. In the vignette below, university-based faculty engage youth as action researchers, mapping community-based resources and examining issues of social justice. It demonstrates the range of potential action research projects as well as the opportunities that exist for collaboration across the educational system.

Methodological Approaches

Although action research is viewed as a cycle or spiral, there are often differences in methods across projects. As mentioned previously, methodological decisions about research design (including data collection and analysis) will flow from the epistemology and conceptual framework of the researcher. Since worldview influences decisions about research topics and questions identified by the action researcher, research methods must also logically fit with the problems posed. At the same time, researchers must be realistic about what they might achieve over the course of a study and consider the logical organization of their studies—will the approaches to data collection provide the necessary data to answer the questions posed? Chapter 3 provides a more detailed discussion about research design.

CHAPTER SUMMARY

- Action research problems can develop from collaborative group or individual inquiry at any level within an educational system.

- There are many strategies individual action researchers and collaborative groups can follow to identify issues to study, including conducting a gap analysis and needs assessment.

- The nominal group technique is useful for soliciting a wide variety of opinions about a topic.

- Critical friends provide action researchers with feedback and support throughout the research process.

- Action researchers can engage in individual research or collaborate with colleagues

through structures that may already exist, including departmental structures, professional learning teams (PLTs) or professional learning communities (PLCs), and virtual research collaboratives.

- For a collaborative action research project to be successful, the group must come to consensus about the focus of study, develop a clear strategy for communicating among group members, and effectively engage stakeholders.

SUGGESTED WEB-BASED RESOURCES

Collaborative Action Research Network (CARN)

https://www.carn.org.uk

Center for Practitioner Research (CFPR)

http://nlu.nl.edu/cfpr

QUESTIONS AND ACTIVITIES

Reflection Questions

1. What are problems related to your everyday practice that you might be able to address through an action research project?

2. Who are some people that may help you with your action research project and support your work?

3. When you think about the gap between the desired situation and what actually is, what issues come to mind?

4. Who might be a critical friend during your action research study?

5. Can you take advantage of organizational structures to support your individual or group action research projects?

Practice Activities

Activity 2A: Examining Your Worldview and Posing a Research Problem

Before embarking on a research project, it is essential that action researchers reflect on their worldview. It is by clarifying this position that research problems may logically flow. This chapter takes the position that the very nature of action research—engaging stakeholders actively in the research endeavor—translates into research that is interpretivist. As such, it is essential to clarify not only the worldview but also the positionality of the researcher in order to clarify how interpretations might be made. Respond to the prompts below in your action researcher journal:

1. When you consider your practice, what are some of the most pressing or significant issues you face? (Jot down as many as you can.)

2. Choose one of the issues you have the power, opportunity, or resources to address. Write this issue down on the center of your paper. Create a web-diagram to jot the stakeholders affected by this issue or contributing to this issue (e.g., students, teachers, administrators, community members, parents; see Figure 2.1, for example). Add your name as a stakeholder. After reflecting on the role you play in contributing to this issue, jot down ways you contribute to or are affected by this issue.

   After mapping out the issue, write about the issue. Why is it important to you? Why does it concern you? What is the history of this issue? What is important contextual information for understanding the issue? How might you make sense of this issue from the frame of your prior personal and professional experiences?

3. Next, write about your ideal situation. What would it look like? What would happen to solve the issue or to improve the situation? What would be the actions of the stakeholders? What would be the effects of these actions?

4. Consider your relationship (or position) relative to the stakeholders you listed. How would you describe each of these positions? For example, how do you engage with these stakeholders? What values do you emphasize as you communicate with the stakeholders? What power dynamics or differences of opinion might be at work?

5. Finally, reread what you wrote and realize that it summarizes your positions as well as your assumptions. How might you use the opportunity to engage in action research to interrogate your assumptions and, perhaps, shift your position? How might you use your action research to better frame the issue you have identified and seek change?

Activity 2B: Completing a Gap Analysis

In order to complete this activity, you need time and space to reflect quietly on your current experiences.

1. Begin by jotting down a list of issues that you confront in your daily work. If you find it difficult to develop this list, you might begin by keeping a journal for one full week, focused on recounting your experiences as a practitioner.

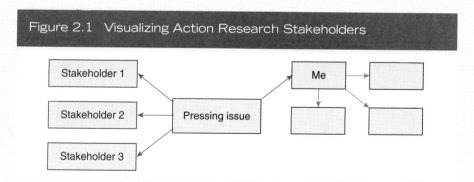

Figure 2.1 Visualizing Action Research Stakeholders

2. At the end of the week, read back over your entries. Does anything stand out as particularly pressing, persistent, or worrisome to you? Use the journal entries to help you create a list of issues.

3. Once you have identified your list, reflect on it carefully. Do you see any patterns? Are there any interconnections between issues listed? Identify one or two topics that you can distill from your list that you would be passionately interested in studying more deeply.

4. Next, divide a sheet of paper into two sections. At the top write "current situation" and on the bottom half write "desired or necessary situation." You can begin at either section to free write about what you see as the current situation or desired situation related to your topic. You can write in prose or create a bulleted list. There are very few rules here; the emphasis should be placed on brainstorming and reflection.

5. Once you have filled both sections of the paper, take a step back to reflect on the gap between the desired and the current situation that you have described. If you are working in a group, allow each member to share one thing they wrote in round-robin fashion. Do not comment on what was written; just use this stage to get ideas out in the open.

6. Finally, consider the implications of the gap you identified. What are factors that might be limiting the desired outcomes from occurring? What might be under your control to change or influence? What do you need more information about? Your answers to these questions could form the basis of a relevant and valuable action research study.

Example Gap Analysis Worksheet

A. Current situation

   {Insert 1 or 2 topics of interest}

   Use space below to describe the current situation relevant to the topic.

B. Desired or necessary situation

   {Insert 1 or 2 topics of interest}

   Use space below to describe the desired situation relevant to the topic.

Journals About Action Research, Teacher Research, Self-Study, and Practitioner Research

Journal Title	Journal URL
Action Learning: Research and Practice	https://www.tandfonline.com/loi/calr20
Action Research	http://arj.sagepub.com/
Journal of Critical Thought and Praxis	http://lib.dr.iastate.edu/jctp/
Journal of Teacher Action Research	http://www.practicalteacherresearch.com/

Open-Access Journals in Education

Journal Title	Journal URL
Educational Action Research	http://www.tandf.co.uk/journals/reac
Educational Research for Social Change	http://ersc.nmmu.ac.za/
i.e.: Inquiry in Education	http://digitalcommons.nl.edu/ie/
Journal of Curriculum and Instruction	http://www.joci.ecu.edu/index.php/JoCI
Networks: An On-line Journal for Teacher Research	http://journals.library.wisc.edu/index.php/networks
Journal of Inquiry and Action in Education	http://digitalcommons.buffalostate.edu/jiae/

Websites About Action Research, Teacher Research, Self-Study, and Practitioner Research

Website Title	Website URL
Collaborative Action Research Network (CARN)	https://www.carn.org.uk
Center for Practitioner Research (CFPR)	http://nlu.nl.edu/cfpr
Self-Study Teacher Research: Improving Your Practice Through Collaborative Inquiry	http://www.sagepub.com/samaras/default.htm
Teacher Research (George Mason University)	https://gse.gmu.edu/research/tr

Planning an Action Research Study

CHAPTER 3

Literature Review and Theoretical Frameworks

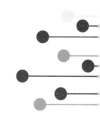

Guiding Questions

1. How knowledgeable are you about the topic of your action research? Where can you find additional information?
2. What role will theory play in guiding your action research?

Keywords and Glossary

Boolean search: a type of search using digital databases in which you clarify your search terms using the operators "AND," "OR," and "NOT" to produce more relevant results.

Critical race theory (CRT): focuses on the primacy of race to define individual and group experiences.

Critical theory: represents a loose confederation of theoretical perspectives concerned with identifying and resisting oppression.

Epistemology: refers to an individual's theory of knowledge.

Feminist theory: draws attention to gender as a social construct.

Interpretivist/constructivist perspective: seeks to understand and interpret observable phenomenon by understanding how knowledge is constructed by individual actors.

Literature review: refers to the systematic process of reading, evaluating, and synthesizing scholarships relevant to a research study.

Postpositivism: holds knowledge as fixed and objective.

Queer theory: refers to a variety of perspectives relating to individual identity that challenge constructs of identity as singular or fixed.

Planning Your Study

Just as in other forms of educational research, an important first step in any action research study is to plan for each stage of the study. The study map shown in Figure 3.1 provides you with a visual resource for drafting a traditional educational research study.

In order to complete the "map," the action researcher begins by brainstorming issues and jots these down in the far left column labeled "Problem or Issue to Be Addressed," then moves on to define the theoretical framework and relevant literature. Next, the researcher drafts research questions and engages in data collection and analysis before finally identifying findings and discussing the importance of these findings. The sections below provide more details about reviewing relevant research literature and identifying the most appropriate theoretical framework. The work you do in this chapter will build on the previous chapters, especially in terms of identifying issues related to practice and in considering your worldview or positionality.

Figure 3.1 Map for Educational Research Study

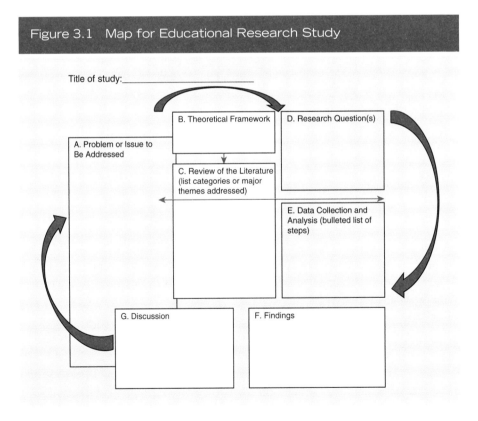

Reviewing Relevant Literature

Identifying a gap or problem in need of study is the first step in an action research study. Consulting relevant educational research literature will help you clarify the problem and determine the best course of action for addressing that problem. Returning to Arlene's study (see Chapter 2), she consulted multiple sources on the topic of culturally responsive instruction, including Geneva Gay's (2002) *Culturally Responsive Teaching: Theory, Research, and Practice* and Gloria Ladson-Billings's (2009) *The Dreamkeepers: Successful Teachers of African American Children*. This background reading led her to critically consider the experiences of her African American students and her relative responsiveness to their needs in the classroom. This led Arlene to develop the topic of her action research project: creating a more culturally responsive curriculum to support student learning. An important part of her action research became improving her ability to develop and deliver culturally relevant instruction. She gathered data and reflected on the effectiveness of this approach to instruction in her classroom. Her review of the relevant literature provided her not only with a rationale for her work but also a guide for action.

The **literature review** is a key component of educational research in general. According to Boote and Beile (2005), "a substantive, thorough, sophisticated literature review is a precondition for doing substantive, thorough, sophisticated research" (p. 3). A literature review is so important for educational research because it helps us connect our work to previous research. "Not understanding the prior research clearly puts a researcher at a disadvantage" (p. 3). The aim of research is to advance understanding and to generate new knowledge. By reviewing previous research literature, we can connect our work to others' and set the context of the study. The literature review also sets the parameters of a study and provides a rationale for the topic and methods of a study.

Seeking Scholarly Sources of Information

Action researchers may begin their search for a topic through a scan of related literature via Google Scholar or research databases available at schools and through libraries. Teachers who are members of professional education groups will also have access to the archives of journals published by the groups. Currently, there are also several open-access educational research journals that may provide relevant studies (see list at the end of Chapter 2). Most public school libraries or media centers will provide educational databases, including ERIC, JSTOR, and Academic Search Complete (EBSCO host). Before you purchase a copy of an article, be sure to consult with the librarian or media specialist at your school or institution. Often you can request copies of articles or books through interlibrary loan if they are not available at your institution.

Identifying Scholarly Literature

There are a variety of sources of information related to teaching and educational issues available online and via websites. It is important to clarify whether these sources are scholarly—that is, based on assertions warranted by empirical evidence and research. In addition to popular news sources and blogs, there are a variety of educational think tanks or foundations that produce position statements about educational approaches. Just as we warn students to check the source, we as action researchers must also critically consider author bias, audience, and claims. An important step is to seek corroborating evidence from other sources and to look for resources published by authors and groups with a significant history in publishing on the subject.

To these ends, it is also important for action researchers to establish criteria for their review of the literature and to share these criteria in the final written report. Documentation might include listing key words used in the search and providing a rationale for the type of sources consulted (or not). Once a topic has been identified, the action researcher can begin building a set of educational hypotheses about that topic. Here the aim is to develop a better understanding of the issue under investigation, including its antecedents and proper context. Based on the understanding of prior research literature, action researchers can move forward with planning their own studies to build on and to extend the existing literature.

Most educational databases allow you to use **Boolean search** techniques. This is a type of search in which you can use signifiers such as "AND" to combine keywords or to delimit your search using "NOT" and "OR." Using Boolean search terms will help you produce more relevant results. Also, it may be valuable to consult the thesaurus of the database you are using to determine appropriate subject descriptors for your search. For example, ERIC recognizes "action research" as a subject descriptor and, according to the ERIC thesaurus, "teacher researchers" and "theory practice relationships" will also searched. You can also use an asterisk in your search to expand the descriptors. For example, when the following search terms were entered into ERIC as subject descriptors—"action research," chang*, and teach* practice—170 results were reported. These results included instances in which "change" or "changing" and "teach" or "teaching" were included as subject descriptors. When in doubt, be sure to consult the research librarian or media specialist at your institution. They can be instrumental in helping you plan out your search. There is also a list of resources to assist you as you conduct your review of the literature at the end of this chapter.

Using Technology to Enhance Your Search

We have already discussed the use of digital databases to guide your review of the literature. There are other digital tools that can help you organize your review of the literature and synthesize your findings. First, it is important to develop a system for organizing and storing your sources. Dropbox and Google Drive provide easy cloud storage of PDFs of articles and other resources that can be accessed anywhere, on any device with Internet access. Mendeley is another tool for organizing PDFs from journals. It will use the metadata from imported documents to generate citations and a bibliography, and Mendeley can also be used to import metadata from databases and search engines to store citations. Similar tools include EndNote, Zotero, and RefWorks. All of these tools have word processing plug-ins that allow you to cite as you write, inserting references from the databases into the body of your paper. This can be tremendously helpful for building your bibliography, especially as you write and revise, adding or removing references. Be sure to check with your librarian to see if you can access these services through your institution before purchasing an account.

Once you have amassed a substantial body of literature, you can use qualitative data analysis software (QDAS), such as Atlas.ti or NVivo, to organize and manage your articles. For example, in NVivo you can import your RefWorks, Mendeley, EndNote, and Zotero libraries. Once the documents are imported, you can create classifications and descriptions for each source (e.g., "methodology," "teaching strategy," "data collection tool") and add memos that briefly describe the literature. From this step, you can code the documents and then link documents by creating "nodes." Eventually, you will be able to create a visual display or "node tree" that enables you to describe the relationships between the sources. This can then launch your writing by serving as an outline for the organization of your review of the literature.

Extending Current Research

Before embarking on a review of the literature, it is important to understand why this is such an important step in your research. Action researchers contribute to educational research by adding to the knowledge base by addressing a gap in the research literature or by replicating a previously conducted study. For action researchers interested in extending current literature by addressing a gap, they are focusing on some aspect of the educational problem that is still not understood or explored. These researchers may be seeking to understand a very narrow part of the larger problem or to move the current research about a topic in a new direction. Sometimes researchers, like Arlene, seek to replicate previously conducted research or integrate new teaching strategies to determine whether they serve to support the unique needs of their classrooms.

In Arlene's case, she chose to adapt strategies described in the literature about culturally relevant teaching into her own classroom. In so doing she not only repositioned herself in a new relationship with her students, but she also entered into a kind of dialogue with the relevant research literature. By testing out aspects of culturally relevant instruction, she was determining its affordances and limitations within the context of her own classroom and practice. While her work was very specific to her context, it can also inform larger understanding about culturally relevant instruction, including describing "lessons learned" and identifying strategies for other teachers to adapt the practices to their own classrooms.

Other action researchers may choose to conduct an even more closely connected replication by adapting the research strategies of other researchers and enacting them in their own classrooms. A well-known example of this approach in the field of the social studies involves an interview protocol referred to as "History Through a Child's Eye" (Bolick, Torrez, & Manfra, 2014). This protocol leads elementary-age students through a series of interview questions designed to help the teacher better assess student understanding of social studies topics. In addition to open-ended questions such as, "What is a president?" and "What is a king?," students are guided through a hands-on activity to sort historical images in chronological order. This protocol has been used by many social studies teachers and researchers to collect data related to student learning outcomes. Borrowing protocols designed by other researchers can provide a good starting point to a new line of inquiry. Research protocols are available in many disciplinary or curriculum fields and in teacher education.

The review of the literature can provide an invaluable source of direction for action researchers. As mentioned above, action researchers may adopt some of the same research strategies discussed in the literature or they may use their review to determine new strategies to explore in their practice. The review of the literature may also help guide the theoretical framing of the study. For example, Arlene adopted a critical race theory approach in her work to integrate culturally responsive instruction and to become an advocate for her African American male students.

Writing the Review of the Literature

The final literature review will provide a critical synthesis of ideas and methods from the field relevant to the topic of study. Rather than just present a laundry list of studies, you will need to compare and contrast across studies and synthesize them at a critical level. In order to do this, you will need to begin by creating a clear organization system. As mentioned above, you can use QDAS to help organize your articles, coding them with key words. It might also be helpful to create an annotated bibliography or a chart of articles that will enable you to quickly compare across your sources (see Activity 3A).

Once you reach a critical mass in your review of articles or saturation (i.e., you no longer encounter new ideas), it is time to begin developing an outline for your literature review. The outline should be organized around big headings, followed by subheadings and more fine-grained topics. Once you have your outline, you can begin developing paragraphs for each heading. One suggestion is to create a separate Word document for each heading, adding quotations and analysis for each topic. The aim for each heading is to clarify what has been done in the field and place the topic in its proper scholarly context. As the synthesis evolves, you will move beyond discussing individual articles or sources toward discussing main ideas that are consistent across the literature. According to Boote and Beile (2005), this synthesis will enable the author to clarify and resolve inconsistencies and tensions in the literature and thereby make a genuine contribution to the state of knowledge in the field, by developing theories with more explanatory and predictive power, clarifying the scope and limitations of ideas, posing fruitful empirical investigations, and/or identifying and pursuing unresolved problems. (p. 7)

Of course, you may also need to describe major debates or dilemmas brought up in research literature as well as uncorroborated evidence.

The review of the literature should also trace the research methods used by others. By considering the strengths and weaknesses of the research methods cited, you can begin to make a case for your action research methods. This may include replicating data collection and analysis methods pursued by other researchers or arguing in favor of new methods altogether.

Finally, a review of the literature may identify a gap in the relevant literature. This would include a discussion about the practical and scholarly significance of the topic under study and areas in need of further study. By noting ambiguities or shortcomings in the relevant literature, researchers uncover new topics of inquiry. As an action researcher, your review of the literature may provide insight about a problem of practice and spark your own study. In the final research report, your review of the literature will provide an argument for your study and outline the logic of your work.

Guiding Theoretical Frameworks

The positionality or worldview and **epistemology** of the researcher will ultimately impact your review of the literature and the direction of the action research project. Egbert and Sanden (2014) refer to epistemology as "the individual lens, created through our worldview that we use to understand knowledge in the world" (p. 17). They argue:

Individuals possess theories about knowledge, whether or not they actively consider them, which results in their thinking in certain ways. Researchers cannot help but bring their beliefs about knowledge, their epistemology, to the forefront and put their understandings about knowledge to use in the ways they conduct their research. (p. 20)

Understanding research in this way means that researchers not only reflect on their epistemologies but must also acknowledge these a priori understandings before undertaking action. According to Merriam (2009),

Getting started on a research project begins with examining your own orientation to basic tenets about the nature of reality, the purpose of doing research, and the type of knowledge to be produced with your efforts. Which orientation is the best fit for your views? Which is the best fit for answering the question you have in mind? (p. 13)

In this vein, there have been three scholarly traditions or paradigms said to describe the very different routes educational researchers might take in their endeavors. They have been identified by van Manen (1975) as the empirical–analytic, interpretive, and critical sciences (see also Armento, 1991) and extended by Merriam (2009) as the positivist/postpositivist, interpretive/constructivist, critical, and postmodern/post-structural (p. 11). For emerging research projects, it is worthwhile to explore these traditions and to identify the framework with the most salience for your topic. Patton (2015) advises, "whatever inquiry framework you choose to use, study the pioneering theorists and more recent practitioners, but study also the critics. There is much to learn, not least of which is where the pitfalls lie in any given approach" (p. 162). Unfortunately, there has often been a conflation of theory and methodology in educational research, contributing to the ambiguity of pinpointing exactly how theory might inform the work of action researchers (see Table 3.1 for representative taxonomies).

Contributing to the complexity of either relying on theory or building theory in educational research is the overall difficulty of conducting educational research. Unlike the hard sciences, educational research focuses on real people, with real issues. The positivist paradigm has been less reliable for the study of human and social phenomena than it has for the study of the natural world. Educational researchers have noted the limitations of positivist paradigms including the difficulty of finding two people with the same experiences and desires, not to mention the fact that people often change their minds or may take a different course of action during a study.

Family of Approaches in Action Research

Perhaps not surprising, then, there is also a lack of consensus regarding the role of theory in action research. Rowell, Riel, and Polush (2016) describe a "family" of action research approaches (theoretical and methodological) that may range between "theory from practice" to "theory into practice." Similarly, McCutcheon and Jung (1990) document "methodological variations of action research" and the manner in which "alternative paradigms," including positivism, interpretivism, and critical science, shape the aims, scope, and methods undertaken in action research studies. They also view action researchers as members of a loosely connected "family" able to accommodate a variety of experiences and epistemological assumptions. "Action research can take on different characteristics because underlying it are different epistemological assumptions, which in turn shape methodological choices as well as how problems are formulated" (p. 150). Similarly, van Manen (1990) acknowledged that "there is no agreed upon set of research techniques or procedures that many or most action research projects and models use" (p. 152).

In other words, there is an ends/means debate about the role of theory within the action research community. Within the literature about action research there is little agreement about whether action research should result in the development of new theories about education based on practice (*ends*) or whether action

Table 3.1 Theoretical Frameworks			
Crotty (1998) epistemologies	Schwandt (2000) epistemological stances	Denzin & Lincoln (2000) paradigms/theories	Merriam (2009) epistemological perspectives
Positivism and postpositivism Interpretivism Critical inquiry Feminism Postmodern, etc.	Interpretivism Hermeneutics Social constructivism	Positivist, postpositivist Constructivist Feminist Ethnic Marxist Cultural studies Queer theory	Positivist/postpositivist Interpretive/ constructivist Critical Postmodern/ post-structural

research emerges from using theory to guide practice (*means*) and, in turn, the study of that practice. This ambiguity, rather than a detriment, should be viewed as opening up new space and opportunity. Action research is oriented in a different direction from more traditional forms of educational research. The focus is on insider perspectives and develops out of concerns emerging from everyday practice (Cochran-Smith & Lytle, 1993, 2009; Stenhouse, Verma, Wild, & Nixon, 1982). As such, the action researcher has a great deal of latitude in determining the scope and direction of the inquiry.

Selected Theories

This relative latitude means that action researchers can and should explore the role of theory in their own work. Below are short descriptions of the theoretical frameworks often referenced in educational research literature (see also Table 3.1). This list is not meant to be exhaustive, but rather informative about the manner in which theories might influence the direction of action research projects.

In this review, the assumption is that the theoretical framework functions like a lens in a camera. It provides a way to focus on an issue and it provides a filter for seeing the topic in a new way. Theory may guide practice and the study of practice or it might be challenged, extended, or replaced by some new theory that emerges from the inquiry process.

Postpositivism

According to Merriam (2009), positivist/postpositivist research perspectives intend to "predict, control and generalize." Here the ontological lens is that knowledge is "objective, external, and out there" (p. 11). The major inquiry approaches nested within this orientation include quantitative methodologies, including experimental, survey, and quasi-experimental designs. While this form of research is often viewed as being "scientific" and therefore generalizable, many action researchers choose not to conduct positivistic research. This is due to the contextual nature of action research and its focus on engaging students as co-constructors of knowledge, rather than passive participants in an intervention. At the same time, action researchers may employ data collection methods associated with positivistic inquiry, including survey methods, and the analysis of quantitative data, including student assessment scores, in their projects.

Interpretivist/Constructivist

The **interpretivist/constructivist perspective** seeks to understand and interpret observable phenomenon by understanding how knowledge is constructed by individual actors. "Interpretive research, which is where qualitative research is most often located, assumes that reality is socially constructed, that is, there is no single, observable reality" (Merriam, 2009, p. 8). As such, there are multiple interpretations that researchers construct based on the data they collect. Researchers follow a naturalistic approach to data collection and analysis and tend to use qualitative techniques to develop "thick descriptions" of social interactions, events, and circumstances. Research is often characterized by "emergent research designs, emic points of view, decentered perspectives, and interpretive analyses" (Miller, Nelson, & Moore, 1998, p. 378). By remaining open to different points of view and perspectives and seeking to understand how participants construct their realities through social interaction, the researcher can develop a more nuanced understanding of human experience.

Critical Theory and Post-Structuralism

Critical theory represents a loose confederation of theoretical perspectives concerned with identifying and resisting oppression. According to Merriam (2009), "Early influences include Marx's analysis of socioeconomic conditions and class structures, Habermas's notions of technical, practical, and emancipatory knowledge, and Freire's transformative and emancipatory education" (p. 9). Post-structuralists are particularly concerned with identifying the relationship between social structures and individual power and authority, especially in terms of understanding how metastructures conscribe individual experiences and undermine individual emancipation. They are often most concerned with economic repression and control and interrogate strategies for reconstructing social structures. Critical research goes beyond describing, toward empowerment and change.

Critical Race Theory (CRT)

Over the decades there has been increasing interest, particularly among scholars of color, to "add different voices to the received wisdom or canon" (Ladson-Billings, 1998, p. 23). Tyson (1986) refers to "race based epistemologies" as part of an overall discussion about issues related to "research, race, privilege, and power in educational research" (p. 40). She contends that the "specificity of oppression" necessitates the creation of theories of knowledge or epistemologies that respond to the inherent nature of racism and racial prejudice. Rather than ascribe to frameworks that are blind to the experiences of people of color, emancipatory epistemologies and liberatory research methodologies must be created.

Critical race theory emerged from critical legal studies and focuses on the primacy of race to define individual and group experiences. According to Delgado and Stefanic (2012),

> The critical race theory (CRT) movement is a collection of activists and scholars interested in studying and transforming the relationship among race, racism, and power. The movement considers many of the same issues that conventional civil rights and ethnic studies discourses take up, but places them in a broader perspective that includes economics, history, context, group- and self-interest, and even feelings and the unconscious. (p. 1)

There are several important tenets or features of CRT, including (1) race is "ordinary" and "part of the common everyday experience of most people of color in this country"; (2) "racism is difficult to cure or address" and color-blind approaches and policies only serve to eradicate the most obvious forms of racial oppression because "large segments of society have little incentive to eradicate it" (also described as interest convergence); (3) race is socially constructed, not biological or genetic; "dominant society racializes different minority groups at different times" (also referred to as "differential racialization"); (4) "everyone has potentially conflicting, overlapping identities, loyalties, and allegiances" ("intersectionality"); and (5) people from traditionally marginalized and underrepresented groups "may be able to communicate to their white counterparts matters that the whites are unlikely to know" (counterstorytelling; see Delgado & Stefanic, 2012, pp. 3–4). From a CRT perspective, research can serve to bring new insights about education reform by focusing primarily on race and racism.

Feminist Theory

Feminist research may draw on a variety of **feminist theoretical** perspectives, depending on the context or specific group of women being studied (see, for example, Lather, 1991, 1996; Reinharz, 1992). In general, "feminist research approaches center on and make problematic women's diverse situations and the institutions that frame those situations" (Creswell, 2013, p. 29). Feminist research may take up postmodern (e.g., Lather, 1991) and post-structural (e.g., Weedon, 1997) critiques of contemporary society to challenge injustice while also maintaining a focus on gender as an essential factor in understanding human experiences. According to Lather (1991), the aim of feminist research is to "correct both the invisibility and distortion of female experience in ways relevant to ending women's unequal social positions" (p. 71). Feminist researchers seek to establish collaborative relationships with participants, to draw attention to gender as a social construct, and to bring about social transformation. According to Stewart (1994), feminist researchers must acknowledge their own positionality while remaining open to understanding the varied experiences of women.

Queer Theory

Queer theory guides an emerging body of scholarship that continues to evolve. Some researchers use postmodern or post-structural orientations to critique dominant discourses surrounding identity, including sexuality and gender. They reject the notion that identity is singular, fixed, or normal (see Watson, 2005). For example, binary categories of gender as female and male or sexuality as heterosexual and homosexual are problematized; these categories are viewed as fluid (Plummer, 2011). Queer theorists "seek to challenge categorization processes and their deconstructions, rather than focus on specific populations" (Creswell, 2013, p. 32). Research that takes on a queer theory lens does not necessarily focus on sexuality or gender; rather, it aims to problematize and reconceptualize taken-for-granted categories of identity and objectification.

Theory and Action Research

These short summaries of various theoretical approaches provide brief introductions to the relevant literature guiding the development of each theoretical framework. It is important to note that, far from being prescriptive, the theorists who developed these frameworks extend an invitation for other researchers to explore phenomena through a variety of lenses. The opportunity for action researchers is to select a theoretical framework as a heuristic to guide inquiry. At the same time, researchers can build upon previous work—to extend it, challenge it, and reframe it. Regardless of the theoretical orientation you adopt, it is important that you engage in a deeper study of the theory and its foundational works.

The role of theory in action research is viewed as being quite different than the role of theory in more traditional forms of educational research (Stringer, 2014). By design, action researchers interrogate knowledge in action. According to Elliott (1991), "It [action research] aims to feed practical judgment in concrete situations, and the validity of the 'theories' or hypotheses it generates depends not so much on 'scientific' tests of truth, as on their usefulness in helping people to act more intelligently and skillfully" (p. 69). Here the perspective of theory as knowledge in action enables researchers to "'re-see' the world, or see through taken-for-granted conceptual categories" (Reason & Bradbury, 2001, p. 451). Action research can result in the deep reflection on preconceived notions about "what works" and might lead to rethinking or reconceptualizing the theories that guide practice and frame professional knowledge. Brause and Mayher (1991) characterize action research as "reflection-in-action":

Teaching practice directly stems from teacher beliefs (implicit or explicit theories); that change in practice depends on change in belief (theory); that the best sources of change in belief (theory) are: reflection-in-action on one's current practice. (p. 23)

By linking theory and practice (since theory is developed through understanding practice), action researchers acknowledge the theories they espouse and through seeking to "explain how and why events occur as they do" end up developing new theories or "ways of incorporating them into mutually acceptable ways of understanding events that enable them to work toward a resolution of the problem investigated" (Stringer, 2014, p. 39). This means that the theories developed through action research are specific to the context in which a problem is being studied. According to Lincoln (1998), "action researchers act on the premises that appropriate action can only be theorized by the community in which the action is to take place; that theorizing about the purposes and outcomes of action is a locally appropriate process" (p. 17). Since theory emerges from practice, it cannot be separated from that practice, nor from the context in which the practice occurs. According to Hendricks (2009), "knowledge is something that action researchers do—their living practice—rather than a fixed, static or absolute entity" (p. 3). So, the theory that emerges from practice is not fixed but rather is emerging, changeable, and iterative.

Action Research Compared to Traditional Educational Research
....

The previous discussion about the role of theory in action research suggests that action research has been conceived of as a distinct form of educational research. These differences include the role of theory and extend to the methods employed. Specifically, in action research, context is not controlled; rather, it is studied in detail to understand its impact on the outcomes (see, for example, Stenhouse et al., 1982). Participants are not chosen at random but are part of the professional (and, perhaps, personal) life of the researcher.

Despite the "family of approaches" associated with action research, proponents often cite the same intellectual grounding for their work in Dewey's (1933, 1938) notions of reflective inquiry and experiential education and Schön's (1983) reflection-in-action (see Hendricks, 2009). For example, change is viewed as a primary aim of action research and many have linked action research to Dewey's pragmatic approach to developing knowledge through action.

There also seems to be fairly widespread agreement about the ways in which action research diverges from other forms of research. Van Manen (1990) points to a set of assumptions identifiable across various forms of action research and offers them as "tentative alternative principles that may be the basis of a more self-reflective human-science form of action research while restoring our relation to children" (p. 152). According to Cochran-Smith and Lytle (1999), this work and others that endeavored to understand appropriate conceptual frameworks for action research resulted in interrelated yet distinctive conceptualizations of the inquiry that included "teacher research as social inquiry, teacher research as ways of knowing within communities, and teacher research as practical inquiry" (p. 17). Similarly, Lincoln (1998) described a "set of shifts" in educational research and argues that action research emerges from "growing understanding among groups of educational researchers that school reform, educational improvement, and social welfare in general are going nowhere without the active participation of those who have in the past been the so-called 'targets' of improvement" (p. 21). In other words, action research engages insiders in the research process to bring about change, whereas other forms of educational research operate from an outside-in approach.

The first step in conducting an action research study is to reflect on your own worldview as well as issues that you are passionately interested in pursuing. You can turn to the research literature for guidance in terms of topics, strategies, and theoretical frameworks that may offer a lens for exploring your issue of study. You must also plan how you will study your problem in a systematic and intentional manner. Chapters 4–8 provide step-by-step guidance for conducting your action research.

CHAPTER SUMMARY

- In order to begin an action research study, there are many conditions researchers must consider, including relevant literature and theoretical issues.

- A researcher's positionality often leads the researcher to explore the relevance of particular theoretical frameworks that align with their worldview.

- In action research, theory is developed in action and through practice. Theoretical frameworks can provide guidance for study in that they offer a "lens" for viewing the world, but they are not meant to be prescriptive.

SUGGESTED WEB-BASED RESOURCES

Mendeley

https://www.mendeley.com/

RefWorks

https://www.refworks.com

Zotero

https://www.zotero.org/

Conducting Research

https://owl.english.purdue.edu/owl/section/2/8/

NVIVO: Tackling the Literature Review

https://www.qsrinternational.com/nvivo/nvivo-community/the-nvivo-blog/tackling-the-literature-review

QUESTIONS AND ACTIVITY

Reflection Questions

1. What new insights do previous studies offer regarding your topic of study?

2. How can you build on, extend, or challenge previous research?

3. As you read about the variety of theoretical frameworks, which seem to stand out to you as relevant to your experiences and work?

Practice Activity

Activity 3A: Conducting a Review of the Literature

1. Identify your research topic and brainstorm related key words or synonyms.

2. Consult with a research librarian or media specialist at your institution. Or if not available, consult the "Conducting Research" page at https://owl.english.purdue.edu/owl/section/2/8/.

3. Write out or document your search strategies in your research journal. You can include this later in your final report.

4. Begin to search online digital databases for relevant articles. Collect these articles as PDFs in Dropbox, Google Docs, or another online database.

5. Annotate your article PDFs using Adobe Acrobat.

6. Code your articles or portions of your article by assigning key words. Here you can use QDAS software such as Atlas.ti or NVivo to map the relationship between articles by creating nodes/trees.

7. A low-tech option: Use sticky notes to list the author, date, and topic of the article or to highlight an important quote or idea. You may also want to include relevant key words. Arrange the sticky notes to create a visual graphic organizer of the literature. Take a picture for safekeeping.

8. Begin to draft your review of the literature. As you write you may want to keep a list of additional information needed. This list will guide your second round of research.

Research Questions and Ethics

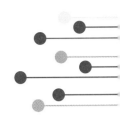

Guiding Questions

1. As you think about your topic, what seems to be a logical strategy for systematically and intentionally studying this topic as part of your day-to-day practice?
2. How can you reframe your research problem as a research question(s)?
3. What data collection approaches will you pursue?
4. How will you protect your participants and maintain high ethical standards in your action research?

Keywords and Glossary

Ethics documentation: refers to the documents that you will share with participants and in your final report to describe the steps you took to engage in ethical action research; may include your personal ethics statement, recruitment documents, and informed consent forms.

Institutional review board (IRB): the governing body that evaluates human subjects research studies before they are implemented to ensure little to no risk for participants.

Qualitative methods: are interpretivist approaches to data collection that provide a thick description of the topic under study, mainly through three approaches: interview, observation, and document analysis.

Quantitative methods: are approaches to data collection that focus on numerical data to understand statistical relationships between variables under study.

Problem Posing: Developing Research Questions

Chapters 1–3 provided suggestions for framing your action research study in terms of scope, scale, focus, and duration. In the initiation stage of a study, the action researcher will consider how broadly or narrowly to define the research problem as well as the granularity of the project. For example, will you focus on a single student, a small group of students, or a single classroom? Or will you cast a wider net to study an entire department, school, or community? The scope and scale of the action research will relate to the purpose and audience of your work. For instance, a teacher endeavoring action research for personal professional development will have a much different set of expectations than a teacher taking part in a school-wide action research initiative. Regardless, it is important to be upfront about expectations and to plan accordingly.

Action research questions emerge from research problems that will frame the course of the action research study. At the end of your study, you will return to your research questions to ensure you have adequately answered the question(s) you posed. It is important to note that research questions may be modified or reframed as the inquiry progresses. Here again, it is helpful to engage peers or "critical friends" to review research questions and to provide feedback.

Activity 4A at the end of this chapter guides you through the process of developing action research questions. Many novice researchers find that initial research questions are too vague or too broad. There are differences between questions that might guide an entire life's work and those that can suitably define a single round of an action research cycle. By posing questions that are both meaningful and practical, action researchers will avoid a great deal of frustration.

In order to begin crafting research questions, reflect on the following questions:

1. What aspect of your practice are you passionately interested in understanding more deeply?

2. Why are you interested in learning more about this part of your practice?

3. What is the relevant literature (including articles, books, web resources, etc.) that you might consult to learn more about the topic?

Once you have clarified your topic, a potential first step may be to simply rephrase the research problem as a question. For example, consider this problem statement:

"I want my students to take a more active role in classroom activities. However, when I integrate cooperative learning activities in my classroom, I am not sure if all students are participating and learning."

This can be reframed as the following research question:

"When I integrate cooperative learning in the classroom, how does it impact student understanding about the topic we are studying?"

After drafting a question or two, the next step is to jot down ways to reasonably collect data to answer the research question(s). The following questions will guide your reflection:

1. How might you intentionally and systematically collect data to help you gain a better understanding of this part of your practice?

2. When could you collect and begin to analyze this data?

3. How can you involve your students, colleagues, peers, and others in your study?

4. Who can help you with your research project?

(See also Activity 4B.)

As you begin to answer these questions, you can refine your research questions as necessary.

Planning for Data Collection

The methods of data collection in action research are similar to other forms of educational research. However, data collection and analysis are ongoing since action research is conceived as a spiral process. Each new understanding leads to new questions and new actions. The cycle of steps or spiral might include look, think, plan, and act (Stringer, 2014) or planning, acting, observing, and reflecting (Kemmis & McTaggart, 2007). In this text, the series of steps include problem posing, action, observation, reflection, and sharing, with data collection and analysis embedded in each step (see Figure 4.1).

Since inquiry is intentionally tied to the daily practice of the action researcher, it often makes the most sense to collect data and interpret meaning during the action and observation phases. For novice action researchers and those working in collaborative research teams, it will be helpful to clarify data collection and individual responsibilities within the project well in advance. Given the iterative nature of action research, it is important for action researchers to also remain open to the possibility that the path of inquiry may shift as a result of new findings over the course of the project.

Choosing Between Qualitative and Quantitative Methods

When you begin to outline your research methods, you will need to determine the most appropriate approach to data collection and analysis. Your methods should align with your research perspective and question(s). As you begin to plan, you need to determine a logical and practical approach to data collection that will provide you with

Figure 4.1   The Action Research Cycle

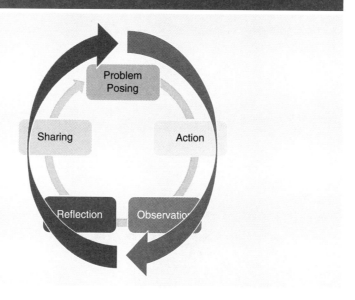

the evidence you need to address the problem(s) you pose in your project. According to Morgan (1998), "for research designs to be practical, they should be (a) reasonably certain to produce fruitful outcomes and (b) ready to be used in a relative routine fashion" (p. 364). Focusing on practical approaches to data collection is particularly important for action researchers since inquiry is integrated into daily practice.

Educational researchers distinguish between qualitative and quantitative methods (e.g., Creswell, 1994; Johnson & Christensen, 2008; see also Table 4.1). Qualitative research is exploratory or descriptive; these studies can help to answer "why" and "how" questions. In this text we focus on the "big three" of **qualitative methods**—observation, interview, and documentary data collection—that are associated with ethnographic and social science research (see Chapter 5). Data are analyzed using open-ended or inductive approaches (see Chapter 6). This means that new theories or hypotheses emerge from data analysis.

Quantitative studies often address questions related to causality and seek to understand numerical patterns in data. **Quantitative methods** include statistical analysis of data within experimental or quasi-experimental studies. Quantitative data are analyzed through a deductive approach (see Chapter 7): 2 sentences is top-down in nature and the researcher tests theories or hypotheses. The quantitative research report will describe statistical relationships between variables.

Decisions about how to approach action research are based on the research problems and questions posed. They refer to the worldview and assumption of the researcher as well as the theoretical framing of the study (Creswell, 1994). For example, if researchers seek emic perspectives, they will pursue research methods

Table 4.1 Qualitative and Quantitative Approaches

Areas of Comparison	Qualitative	Quantitative
Perspectives	Interpretivist, critical Broad Exploratory, descriptive Emic	Positivist Narrow Confirmatory, focused Etic
Data types	Verbal data Observation field notes Interviews or focus groups Artifacts or work samples Researcher journals	Numerical data Assessment data Survey or questionnaire data
Data analysis	Inductive Coding	Deductive Statistical analysis
Potential limitations	Large amount of data	Requires large sample size

to understand insider perspectives and culturally relevant meanings. On the other hand, an etic perspective refers to objective or outsider perspectives about a phenomena. In general, qualitative methods are more commonly associated with an emic perspective. This is because qualitative methods emerge from interpretivist or critical perspectives and quantitative methods emerge from positivist/postpositivist perspectives (see Chapter 2).

Qualitative and quantitative methods can be combined in mixed methods studies (Creswell & Plano, 2007; see also Chapter 7). Mixed method studies can follow a variety of approaches based on priority and sequential decisions (Morgan, 1998). For example, qualitative data analysis could form the basis for a quantitative study by providing insight about content for interventions or surveys and questionnaires. Quantitative data analysis could provide initial findings (e.g., from a survey or assessment test data) to guide a more in-depth, ethnographic study of a sample of participants. It is important when making decisions about mixed methods to consider complimentary approaches that are logical and practical.

Ethical Concerns

Regardless of the methodological approaches pursued, action researchers must take into consideration ethical concerns associated with conducting research involving human subjects (see also McNiff & Whitehead, 2010; Zeni 2001). While much has been written about the ethics of educational research and action research more specifically, the simple guideline is to *do no harm*. According to McNiff and Whitehead (2010) in their introduction to action research,

Ethics is about how to live a good life; in other words, how to live a life that is conducted in accordance with our values. . . . Do the best you can, with honesty and humility, which is all you or anyone else can ask of you. (p. 80)

They recommend action researchers take the following steps:

1. Draw up your **ethics documentation** to include an ethics statement and letters requesting and granting permission.

2. Negotiate access with principals, participants, parents, and other caregivers.

3. Promise confidentiality.

4. Ensure participants can withdraw from the research.

5. Ensure good professional and academic conduct.

6. Keep good faith (McNiff & Whitehead, 2010, pp. 76–79; see also pp. 81–85 for example documentation).

Following these steps will help to ensure that you conduct ethical research; it will also lay the foundations for a successful project.

The Ethics of Control Groups

Before planning to conduct a quasi-experimental study, you should consider the ethical implications. For instance, many beginning action researchers often intend to designate one class or group of students as an "experimental" class and the other as a "control" class during their studies. This approach poses both methodological and ethical issues (see Morgan & Morgan, 2009, for a full comparison of group designs and single-case research methods). First, it is very difficult to compare students, even students in similar grades and achievement levels. Educational researchers use a variety of complex statistical analyses to create *matched samples* based on probable statistical similarities between students. At the same time, it is unethical for a teacher to withhold a teaching method or resources to a group of students (in this case the control group) if she believes them to be beneficial. Therefore, consider instead collecting baseline data and then compare student outcomes by analyzing before and after data. It may be necessary to try out new teaching strategies or other practices multiple times. Students may need appropriate scaffolding before experiencing success with new teaching and learning approaches. For example, a teacher transitioning from a teacher-centered, lecture-based classroom to a more student-centered, inquiry-based classroom should use care to ease the transition for students.

It is recommended that teachers integrate the study of new techniques over multiple weeks and units. For example, a teacher interested in engaging students with cooperative learning activities such as the jigsaw method might plan for research like the following:

Week 1 (baseline): Class A and class B – no cooperative learning

Week 2: Class A and class B – with cooperative learning

Week 3: Class A and class B – with cooperative learning

Week 4: Class A and class B – with cooperative learning

In such a scenario, the teacher may be able to draw conclusions about the impact of the new approach on student learning outcomes while also developing a better understanding about how her teaching practices evolved over time. Using this single-case, longitudinal approach, she will be able to respond to student needs during the various action phases of her project. Considering the step-by-step process of conducting action research, as well as identifying potential ethical issues, is an important part of the planning process and should be included in the research plan of a study.

Institutional Review Boards

Many university-based researchers will already be familiar with **institutional review boards** (IRBs) and the IRB process of proposing and seeking approval for university or institutional-sanctioned "human subjects research." Most school districts also have requirements for seeking approval before conducting research in classrooms and with students. Be sure to consult relevant administrative bodies early in the planning phase of the research process.

In many cases, requests by teachers to conduct research in their own classrooms, with their own students, may be considered "exempt." This is due to the nature of teaching as inquiry and the way in which teachers are often expected to reflect on and revise instruction. Nonetheless, it is important to acknowledge and plan for ways to mitigate risks associated with conducting such research. For example, although teacher action researchers can take steps to ensure confidentiality, for instance, by using pseudonyms in final reports or presentations, it may be difficult to completely mask the school in which the teacher conducted her research. In these situations the action researcher will need to do as much as possible to protect the identity of participants as well as to explain to them the risk of participating. The action researcher must go through the requisite steps of vetting the research plan in advance before beginning an inquiry.

Transparency and openness are important in the early stages of action research, particularly when recruiting participants and seeking parental consent. By working with administrators and district-level supervisors, classroom teachers can navigate the process of seeking approval for their important work as action researchers. In no way should these steps be viewed as insurmountable. They simply help to ensure that the action researcher and participants are protected. You may even find the process of proposing research projects to IRBs as beneficial in helping to develop high-quality action research plans. In many ways, it is the first step in the peer review process.

CHAPTER SUMMARY ●————————————————————

- Action research questions must be manageable to be effective.

- Action research methods can be qualitative or quantitative.

- Methods decisions should appropriately reflect the worldview of the researcher, the theoretical framing of the study, and the aim of the project.

- Action researchers are responsible for conducting ethical studies that do no harm to participants.

- Action researchers must develop their plans for data collection and ethics documentation in advance of the study.

QUESTIONS AND ACTIVITIES ————————————————

Reflection Questions

1. What are you passionately interested in studying?

2. How can you frame your interest, problem, or issue related to practice as a question?

3. What data collection methods are most appropriate to your study?

4. How will you protect your participants?

Practice Activities

Activity 4A: Crafting an Action Research Question

Crafting a good action research question is an important first step in any project. Although the question may change over time, it provides the foundation for developing a research plan and methods. Begin by jotting down questions that immediately come to mind about a topic of interest to you as a practitioner. If you have a hard time coming up with questions, you might work through various types of questions: who, why, what, where, when, and how?

Below is an example of a strategy for posing questions to narrow a research problem or interest into a more manageable research question. This protocol is designed to be interchangeable with other topics; simply insert relevant language for your work.

Topic: Integration of computer technology

- Who is using technology in the school? (Are students using technology in the school? Are teachers using technology in the school?)

- Why are people using computer technology in the school? (Why are teachers using computer technology? Why are students using computer technology?)

- What kinds of technology are being used? (Are kids and teachers using the same kinds of technology?)

- Where is technology being used? (Is technology being used in the classroom? Is technology being used in core subjects? Is technology being used in computer labs?)

- When is technology being used? (Is technology being used as part of the regular school day? Is technology being used after school? Are students required to use technology to complete assignments? Do teachers use technology during the day?)

- How is technology being used in the school? (How is technology being used consistently every day? How is technology readily available? How successful is the integration of technology?)

After jotting down questions, critically analyze your questions to determine whether the questions raised are under your control and whether you could answer the question in a reasonable fashion. Based on your analysis, refine the questions by narrowing the scope or clarifying the focus.

- Are teachers integrating computer technology in the classroom? Why?

- To what extent does this use impact student learning?

Are teachers integrating computer technology in the language arts classroom to teach writing?

To what extent does this impact student writing skills?

How are teachers integrating student-authored blogs in the language arts classroom to teach persuasive writing?

To what extent does this impact student persuasive writing skills?

Activity 4B: Preliminary Research Plan

Answer each question in narrative form.

1. What aspect of your practice are you passionately interested in understanding more deeply?

2. Why are you interested in learning more about this part of your practice?

3. What is the relevant literature (including articles, books, web resources, etc.) that you might consult to learn more about the topic?

4. How might you intentionally and systematically collect data to help you gain a better understanding of this part of your practice?

5. When could you collect and begin to analyze this data?

6. How can you involve your students, colleagues, peers, and others in your study?

7. How will you protect your participants? (ethics documentation)

8. Who can help you with your research project?

9. What questions and concerns do you have about conducting your own study?

Activity 4C: Critical Friends

Share your preliminary research plan with your critical friends and request feedback.

Note: "Critical" in the context of the group is intended to mean "important" or "key" or "necessary." The critical friends process provides an opportunity to both solicit and provide feedback in a manner that promotes reflective learning. For the purposes of this assignment, you should address the action research plan shared by your colleague and give feedback that is both warm (positive) and cool (critical). The feedback should be given in a supportive tone and discussants should provide practical suggestions. For example, what are strengths of the action research plan? What are suggestions for moving forward or improving? Can you offer practical advice based on your experiences? Do you have suggestions about resources to share?

Collecting and Analyzing Data

CHAPTER

5

Qualitative Approaches to Data Collection

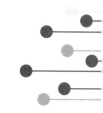

Guiding Questions

1. Once you have identified a research question, what is the most logical approach for collecting data to answer your question?
2. What are the three major approaches to qualitative data collection in action research?
3. How can you integrate data collection into your daily practice?

Keywords and Glossary

Active listening: refers to techniques whereby a researcher explicitly focuses attention on a participant and probes for understanding during an interview or other data collection event, through thoughtful listening, checking for understanding, and prompting for more information.

Field notes: are created as researchers jot down notes during qualitative observations. They may be open-ended, resembling ethnographic field notes, or be guided by an observation protocol.

Focus group interviews: refer to interviews that include two or more participants and often no more than seven to 10 participants. They are used to capture "group think" and are most suitable for understanding public or shared experiences.

Interview protocol: is a written guide of interview questions that are usually aligned very closely with the research question(s) and provide the researcher with a roadmap to follow over the course of the interview.

Memos: can be used by researchers in early data collection and analysis to begin to make connections between pieces of data. They may originate from the action researcher's journal and should be carefully stored and archived for future analysis.

Qualitative data collection: includes interpretivist approaches to data collection that seek to provide a thick description of the topic under study, mainly through three approaches: interview, observation, and document analysis.

Semistructured interview protocols: provide some guidance for interviews or observations without being overly rigid. Interview questions and protocols align closely with the action research question(s).

Think-aloud protocols: are often used in teaching to model metacognitive approaches and may be used in action research as a tool to understand participant experiences, including learning strategies and understandings.

Triangulation: refers to the process of collecting multiple forms and types of data during a research study. It is said to improve the trustworthiness of findings.

Chapter Overview

As discussed in previous chapters, action research aligns most closely with interpretivist, constructivist, and critical approaches to educational research. Qualitative approaches to data collection fit best with these approaches since they will provide the necessary data for creating thick descriptions of the problem or topic under study. It is important to keep in mind that data collection will occur throughout the phases of the action research process as described in Figure 5.1.

For example, the action researcher may want to interview stakeholders or conduct observations throughout the process of problem posing, action, observation, reflection, and sharing. Unlike more traditional research approaches that follow a linear approach, here data collection is ongoing. This is due to the nature of action research; it is embedded in the site of inquiry and the inquiry is about everyday practice, so there is no appropriate time to start or end the inquiry. Rather, data collection is immersive and total. The action researcher is seeking to understand her practice and to bring about change; throughout the process, she gathers evidence to understand the impact of her work. Referring to the reflexive nature of action research, McNiff and Whitehead (2010) ask, "Are you [the action researcher] clear about the relationships between your own learning and other people's learning, and how these potentially inform your and their actions?" It is important to clarify your intentions before embarking on a project.

Figure 5.1   The Action Research Cycle

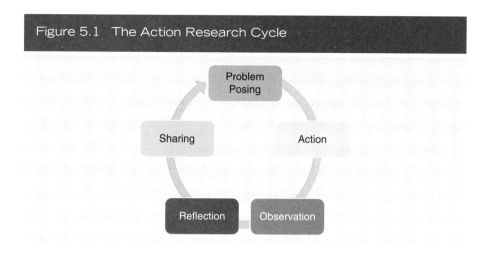

At the same time, it may not be practical or realistic to engage in constant data collection and analysis. For example, action researchers may have deadlines for producing a final report or sharing findings. It might also be helpful for novice researchers and collaborative action researchers to focus on data collection during the action and observation phases in order to make the project more manageable to individual contributors.

Qualitative Data Collection

In qualitative data collection, evidence often comes from three main forms of data: interview, observation, and artifacts. Each form of data collection is described below. For each, there are a variety of choices the action researcher can make. It is important to remain attuned to the purpose of your inquiry as you make methodological decisions. By putting your research questions front and center (perhaps even literally on an index card or sticky note), you will make methodological decisions that will help you build a trustworthy action research project.

Interviews

One of the most common approaches to qualitative data collection is to conduct one-on-one interviews with participants. This form of data collection provides a rich opportunity to learn about individual experiences and perspectives and is mainly "designed to elicit depth on a topic of interest" (Namey & Trotter, 2015, p. 453). Interviews used for educational research are different than a typical television or talk-show interview. Rather than entertain at the expense of the person being interviewed, interviews in action research seek to build relationships and to develop understanding about the participant's point of view and experiences.

The aim here is to develop an emic perspective and to ultimately develop empathy or the ability to take on another's perspective. Qualitative interviews are both conversational and systematic. According to Namey and Totter (2015), in-depth interviews "are conducted one-on-one, use open-ended questioning, use inductive probing to get depth, and look and feel like a conversation" (p. 453). Here the action researcher engages in conversation with participants to gain understanding specific to the research problem posed in the project. According to Patton (2015), "we interview people to find out from them those things we cannot directly observe and to understand what we've observed" (p. 426). The aim is to understand other peoples' stories and to discover more about their perceptions and experiences.

There are many benefits to conducting interviews. Researchers can gather in-depth data relatively quickly. There is also the potential for following up with participants to probe for more detailed understanding. When combined with other forms of data collection such as observations, interviews provide insight about individual perspectives, perceptions, and experiences (Marshall & Rossman, 2016).

In action research projects, researchers may choose to interview key informants who can help them learn more about their own work and the impact it has on others. This might include a teacher interviewing her students, administrators, colleagues, or parents. School administrators might choose to interview teachers, students, or members of other stakeholder groups. Of course, deciding whom to interview depends on the research questions posed and the topic under study. For example, an action researcher interested in program evaluation might interview program participants and facilitators to determine the extent to which the program is meeting its goals. An action researcher interested in learning more about the effectiveness of a pedagogical strategy in her classroom would need to interview her students to understand the impact on student experiences.

Interviewing for Classroom Teachers

For classroom teachers, the notion of conducting interviews may seem daunting. However, you should not be dissuaded from this approach to data collection. Since the aim of action research is to ultimately change and improve practice, interviews provide the opportunity to gain valuable information necessary to bring about change. By interviewing students, teachers truly have an opportunity to become students of their students. By giving students a voice in the research process, they affirm the importance of their students and the knowledge they possess. By interviewing colleagues, administrators, and parents, teachers can identify important issues and learn more about the context in which they are teaching. They may also be able to identify best practices and new strategies. Even a short, 5-minute interview can yield important data on which to build an understanding about the experiences and outcomes of students and other key participants. Conducting interviews is just one example of the way in which action research can be transformative for both teachers and their students.

Benefits for Interview Participants

At the same time, there are many potential benefits for participants who take part in an interview. For instance, in the fields of counseling and physical and mental health there has been much discussion about the therapeutic effects of interviews on participants. It appears that through the process of talking about lived experiences, participants become attuned to understandings they previously had not considered or it simply feels good to talk about a difficult or challenging experience. Motivational interviewing has been used in health sciences to gently probe participants toward making healthier choices through raising awareness of prior experiences and options for new behaviors. In educational research it is common to use a think-aloud approach to monitor student understanding and probe for metacognition (see, e.g., Van Someren, Barnard, & Sandberg, 1994). Participating in a think-aloud may be educative for students as they become aware of their own understandings, gain exposure to new content, and develop a better sense of metacognitive techniques.

Steps in the Interview Process

Although interviews feel familiar in form, there are important steps action researchers must take to ensure that they collect high-quality information through interviews. The value of an interview is largely dependent on the quality of the questions asked. According to Patton (2015), "skilled interviewing is about asking questions well so that interviewees want to share their stories" (p. 427). Keys to good interviewing include creating an **interview protocol** or list of questions in advance of the interview, establishing rapport with the participant, recording responses, and developing **active listening** skills.

Interview Protocol. An interview protocol is a written guide of interview questions. These are usually aligned very closely with the research questions and provide the researcher with a roadmap to follow over the course of the interview. They prompt the researcher to ask questions in a focused and logical manner. They also help to maintain the pace of the interview and the proper direction. In typical qualitative interview protocols, the researcher guides the participant through a series of questions focused on a particular topic and designed to reveal participants' experiences and perspectives about the topic. According to Marshall and Rossman (2016), the typical method of designing interview protocols "is based on an assumption fundamental to qualitative research: The participant's perspective on the phenomenon of interest should unfold as the participant views it (the emic perspective), not as the researcher views it (the emic perspective)" (p. 150).

Even within the emic perspective, there are varying degrees of control the interviewer may wish to exert over the direction of the interview conversation. Roulston (2010), for example, refers to six broad "conceptions of qualitative interviews" (p. 203), ranging from interviews that produce "objective" knowledge to those that lead to "collaborative, transformative relationships with research participants" (p. 224). Patton (2015) categorizes interview "instrumentation" as (1) "informal conversational interview," (2) "interview guide approach," (3) "standardized open-ended interview," and (4) "closed, fixed response interview" (p. 438). Marshall and Rossman (2016) add "constructed, or dialogic, interview" to the list of interview types (p. 150).

The approach to interviewing and the design of the interview protocol will be shaped by the epistemology or worldview of the researcher and the aim of the research project. For example, Kvale and Brinkmann (2009) refer to two different metaphors of the interviewer as either an "industrious miner digging for nuggets of objective facts" or "the intrepid traveler, the interpreter of reality seeking a depth of engagement" (pp. 48–50). In other words, the perspective of the interviewer as a fact seeker or co-constructor of knowledge will yield very different approaches to data collection.

Interview Approaches. Depending on the approach to interviewing followed, researchers may develop structured or **semistructured interview protocols** or leave the interview questions completely open. As the names suggest, the more structured protocols include a series of questions from which the interviewer plans not to deviate, whereas the semistructured or open-ended approaches provide varying degrees of openness regarding the course of the interview. There are benefits to the different types of interviews and the researcher must make choices in advance about the trade-offs about each approach. For example, a structured interview protocol might be beneficial to action researchers working in research teams when they want to be sure to ask the same questions across the team or if they are working with many participants. Yet at the same time, researchers who follow a closed or fixed-response interview may miss important opportunities for data collection.

Semistructured and open-ended interviews leave much more room for developing rapport, trust, and collaboration with the interview participant. Open-ended interviews are conversational in nature and allow the researcher to follow the story or conversation as it enfolds with little expectation of how the interview should go. They "capture the data in the vernacular and in context" (Guest, Namey, & Mitchell, 2013, p. 93), they may occur on the spot, and they are often "spontaneous and serendipitous" (Marshall & Rossman, 2016, p. 150). Yet for novice researchers it might be difficult to gather appropriate data from interview episodes without at least some guiding questions. According to Namey and Trotter (2015), semistructured or structured interviews "provide data relevant to the research objectives" while also taking "the encounter into a research mode that decreases some aspects of the natural context" (p. 450). Table 5.1 provides more details about the various types of interviews.

According to Forsey (2012), "how one conceptualizes a research approach obviously helps determine the style of interview pursued" (p. 366). It is important, then, for action researchers to acknowledge their own perspectives regarding research as well as the purposes of their work and allow their data collection to follow.

Table 5.1	Interview Types
Structured	Closed protocol; interview does not deviate from the schedule of questions across multiple participants and interview episodes; management of participant responses; data analysis is simplified since responses can be easily compared.
Semistructured	Generally includes 3–5 questions (often the opening and closing questions) across all interview episodes; interview can deviate from the schedule of questions based on participant responses; generally aims to ask all of the questions on the schedule; includes open-ended questions; facilitation of participant responses through probing questions and openness about the direction of the interview.
Open-ended	Questions posed during interviews are open-ended and more informal, there may be a great deal of variability across the interviews and with multiple participants; the tone of the interview is more casual and conversation; co-construction of knowledge between interviewer and participant is valued.

Interview Rapport. Regardless of the approach to interviewing that the action researcher chooses, establishing rapport in the first interactions with the participant is essential. It is important to set a positive tone for the interview and to reduce the anxiety of the participant from the outset. This might involve describing the goals for the interviews and completing release forms/informed consent forms. Fortunately, for action researchers they will often know the participants they are interviewing. Since establishing trust is an important element for interviews, they must remain aware of the ways in which prior relationships (e.g., student–teacher, teacher–administrator) might impact the direction of interviews.

Over the course of the interview, the action researcher should remain nonjudgmental and ask open-ended questions whenever possible. Skilled researchers know when to ask follow-up questions and to probe for deeper understanding and when to allow interview participants to guide the direction of the interview. According to Patton (2015), probes are used to deepen the response to a question, increase the richness and depth of responses, and give cues to the interviewee about the level of response that is desired" (p. 464). Simple techniques for probing include asking "detail-oriented probes" (who, what, where, when, and how questions), "elaboration probes" (nonverbal cues such as head nodding or encouraging comments), "clarification probes" (to clarify something that is ambiguous), and "contrast probes" (asking the participant to make comparisons; Patton, 2015, pp. 465–466). The aim across all of these probes is to enhance communication between the interviewer and participant.

Recording Responses. Action researchers must also contend with decisions about how best to record interviews. Some may choose to use an electronic recording device and others may prefer to take notes by hand. Again, there are trade-offs to both approaches. For example, an electronic recording device increases the chances of being able to create a verbatim transcription of the interview, and some argue that it is less distracting to the participant (Forsey, 2012). Taking written notes during an interview can be distracting to participants, but it provides a good backup in case the electronic device fails to record. Depending on the length of the interview, action researchers may be able to wait until the interview is over to jot down notes or to write a reflection about the interview. Regardless of the approach taken, interviews should be treated as data collection events and every effort must be made to collect and record the data in a thoughtful and conscientious manner. This will ensure that data analysis will go more smoothly and also protect the interview participant. Any text or audio files gathered over the course of an interview should be properly labeled and archived. Most IRBs require that related files are stored on a secure, password-protected device.

Developing Active Listening. Perhaps one of the most difficult skills for action researchers to develop is active listening. According to Seidman (2006), it is important to "listen more, talk less" (p. 78). During an interview, it is often hard to really listen to the participant while also trying to think about the next question to ask. It is also difficult to allow for times of silence or "wait time." According to Patton (2015), "you, as the interviewer, must maintain awareness of how the interview is flowing, how the interviewee is reacting to questions, and what kinds of feedback are appropriate and helpful to maintain the flow of communication" (p. 467). Active listening techniques can help the interviewer remain focused on the participant while also probing for deeper understanding. Seidman (2006) argues that "interviewers must listen on at least three levels": (1) they must listen intently in order to "internalize what participants say," (2) they must listen for the "inner voice" of participants, and (3) they "must listen while remaining aware of the process as well as the substance" of the interview episode (pp. 78–79). There is far more going on in an interview for data collection than in a regular conversation. Action researchers must be able to balance the line between maintaining a conversational tone, while probing for understanding. Active listening within the context of qualitative interviews might include strategies to support and reinforce participants' responses (Patton, 2015, p. 467), including "words of thanks, support, and even praise will help make the interviewee feel that the interview process is worthwhile and support ongoing rapport" (p. 467).

Wrapping Up the Interview. Often researchers will add a final question, such as "What question do you wish I had asked or should I have asked?" or "Do you have anything else to add?" These final, open-ended questions will provide participants the final word and might reveal concerns that the interviewer had not previously conceived. In addition, it is important for the interviewer to encourage participants to follow up if they think of any additional, pertinent information. You may also assure participants that you will provide copies of the interview transcript for their review.

Summary on Interviews

Through careful planning and by remaining cognizant during the interview, action researchers can use interviews to explore "the complexities and contradictions of social life in schools and beyond" (Forsey, 2012, p. 374). Interviews are rich sources of data that provide the opportunity to learn more about individual experiences in ways not afforded by other data collection techniques. "We interview in order to find out what we do not and cannot know otherwise" (p. 364)—that is, the inner thoughts and experiences of our participants. As a data collection tool for action researchers, interviews can have a powerful impact on the researcher. For example, as a teacher interviews her students, she may become aware of information about her students she did not previously know. By taking the time to provide "voice" to her students, she empowers them to become a part of not only the research endeavor but an active member of the community of practice in the classroom.

At the same time, there are limits to interviews as data collection tools. "In some cases, interview partners may be unwilling or uncomfortable sharing all that the interviewer hopes to explore" (Marshall & Rossman, 2016, p. 151). There may be some cases when interview participants do not feel it is safe to be completely truthful, for example, in the case of vulnerable populations, such as undocumented immigrants. There may be times when interview participants cannot articulate what they are thinking and feeling or may misunderstand the questions being asked. "Children may tell you what they think what you want to hear" (Koshy, 2010, p. 88). In some instances, researcher bias and perspective may prohibit asking questions in a way that probes for the participants' perspectives. For all of these reasons, it is very important that interviewers establish rapport with participants and seek out other opportunities for data collection to confirm or corroborate interview responses.

Focus Group Interviews

Focus group interviews engage at least two or more participants in group interviews; they typically include seven to 10 people who do not know each other but share a common experience (Marshall & Rossman, 2016). This approach to data collection is most appropriate when the researcher hopes to gain an understanding of the manner in which a phenomenon or experience is socially constructed by participants. Focus groups can capture "group think" and are suitable for understanding public or shared experiences.

Focus groups do not have to be formal. It may be difficult for action researchers to gather a group of people who do not know each other. Since the aim of action research is to understand an issue related to practice, it may be helpful for action researchers to engage stakeholder groups that are familiar with the topic of research to directly engage with each other. For example, teachers may turn whole-class discussions or circle-time into a kind of focus group and administrators might use portions of professional learning team (PLT) meetings or faculty meetings as an opportunity to collect data through a series of guiding questions.

The aim of the focus group interview is to ask "focused questions to encourage discussion and the expression and differing opinions and points of view" (Marshall & Rossman, 2016, p. 154). Unlike one-to-one interviews, focus groups engage participants in listening and responding to each other's opinions. "This method assumes that an individual's attitudes and beliefs are socially constructed" (p. 154). Here, qualitative data collection is "a social experience" (Patton, 2015, p. 475) in which participants interact with each other and, through the process, come to deeper understanding about their own experiences. Participants have the opportunity to hear other participants respond to interview questions and this may or may not extend their answers.

Approaches to Focus Groups

Just as there are different approaches to conducting interviews, there is a range of approaches to conducting focus groups. Again, the perspective of the researcher, the aim of the qualitative inquiry, and the researcher questions will drive the choice about whether to use a focus group and, if so, the approach taken. Patton (2015) outlines 12 "varieties" of focus groups (see p. 476). For action researchers, the following varieties may be most appropriate:

- Research focus group: "Interview with a small group of relatively similar people (homogeneity sampling) on a specific topic of research interest."

- Evaluation focus group: "Interview with a group of program participants to get their perspectives on and experiences with a specific program."

- Diversity-focused group: "Interview people with diverse perspectives and experiences regarding some issue to compare and contrast their perspectives as they interact."

- Convergence-focused group: "Interview people with relatively homogenous experiences to identify commonalities and shared patterns."

- Group interviews with naturally occurring or existing groups: "Interviews with . . . members of any already existing group of any kind."

- Dyadic interviews: "Two interviewees interact together in response to open-ended research questions." (p. 476)

Strengths of Focus Groups

There are many strengths and affordances of conducting focus groups. Since they involve multiple participants, they afford the opportunity to interview more participants, more efficiently. They also can highlight diverse perspectives within a group. In order to function properly, focus groups must be planned carefully to create "a permissive nonthreatening environment" that enables participates "to share perceptions and points of view without pressing participants to vote or reach consensus" (Krueger & Casey, 2009, p. 4). Since focus groups allow for interactions among participants, they may also enhance the quality of data collection. For example, Krueger and Casey (2009) contend that focus group members often provide checks on each other, preventing extreme or false views. The researcher has an opportunity to not only hear interview responses, but observe the interactions among the group members, including nonverbal responses.

Choosing Between Interviews and Focus Groups

The research topic and question will guide the mode of inquiry and methodological decisions about data collection techniques. Each of the modes of inquiry and data collection techniques has affordances and limitations. For instance, it is much more difficult to maintain the confidentiality of participants in a focus group. Therefore, action researchers should use caution when engaging these methods for sensitive topics. At the same time, it is difficult to assert individual experiences in a focus group, particularly if some participants dominate the discussion or choose not to participate actively. According to Patton (2015), "those who realize that their viewpoint is a minority perspective may not be inclined to speak up and risk negative reactions [within a focus group]" (p. 478). Table 5.2 compares the affordances of interviews and focus groups (adapted from Namey & Trotter, 2015, p. 454).

In general, interviews are more suitable for understanding focused or narrow research topics and individual experiences, whereas focus groups can help to capture information about broader topics, especially public events, and group dynamics.

Table 5.2 Common Uses of Interviews and Focus Groups

Interview	Focus Groups
• For narrower topics that require depth	• For broader topics that require range
• If interested in personal narratives and individual experiences or opinions	• When studying social norms or seeking public-level narratives
• To understand connections and relationships between particular events, phenomena, and beliefs	• If interested in group dynamics or process
• For highly sensitive or highly personal topics	• To develop or pretest campaigns or messages
• When response independence is important	• To evaluate processes, programs, or messages
	• As a way to "member check" findings from participant observations and in-depth interviews

Of course, the reality for most action researchers is that it may be necessary to remain flexible and open to potential data sources however they may appear. Being opportunistic may be an important practical approach to accounting for differences across a sample and gathering data during real-time practice. According to McNiff and Whitehead (2010), "The only sensible rule for selecting any particular method is that it enables you to find out what you want to know better than another. Follow your common sense and sensitivities about the appropriateness of each kind" (p. 155). Common sense will guide the direction and path of inquiry and begins in the planning stages.

Planning for Interviews and Focus Group Interviews

Once the researcher has determined which approach to collecting interview data will be most methodologically sound, she should plan for the interview by creating an interview protocol. The protocol can be based on the research topic and questions. It may also build on previous interviews or data collection episodes.

Steps for Developing an Interview Protocol

In order to develop an interview protocol, the action researcher must remain cognizant of the aims of the inquiry and the research question(s) posed. Some researchers include the research question(s) in the protocol as a useful reminder about the purpose(s) of the study. Generally, interview protocols are between five and 10 questions designed to help guide the interview or protocol. Often members of an IRB will ask to review a copy of the protocol as part of their process of vetting human-subjects research, and the interview protocol should be attached to the end of final research reports as an appendix. Interview protocols may include demographic or biographical questions (e.g., educational background, school/work experience, interests, hobbies). The questions should build in a logical fashion to elicit an understanding of experiences with the topic of study and to gain insider knowledge from participants. A good final question for a research protocol is to ask, "What else should I know about your experience with [insert your topic of study]?" You will create an interview protocol in the activities below by following a step-by-step guide.

Think-Aloud Protocol

Since many action researchers are interested in understanding experiences as well as outcomes for participants, a **think-aloud protocol** might be a useful tool for probing for understanding. Traditionally used by teachers to model metacognitive strategies for students (e.g., the teacher thinks out loud as she reads through a piece of text, pausing to make metacognitive comments), think-alouds can be retooled as a data collection device. This might include guiding students through a series of exercises to probe for their understanding about specific content or to assess their skills. For example, a think-aloud strategy has been used in historical education research to capture student reasoning and historical thinking skills (Van Someren, Barnard, & Sandberg, 1994). A think-aloud could be embedded into regular instruction as a means for formative assessment and as a data collection tool. Think-alouds can also be integrated into both individual interviews and focus group interviews and become part of the interview protocol.

Transcription Practices

As mentioned above, interviews and focus groups will provide a great deal of information for action researchers. It is recommended that they are recorded either using an electronic device or through written notes. After data collection occurs, audio recordings and written notes should be transcribed into long form. Verbatim transcriptions are ideal, and researchers should endeavor to transcribe as soon after the interview occurs as possible, while memories of the event are still fresh. I recommend a two-column note format for researchers interested in coding by hand. It is OK to use abbreviations in transcriptions as long as they are used consistently and will be readily apparent during data analysis. There has been some debate about whether or not it is important to also capture nonverbal cues in interview transcriptions—for instance, pauses, sighs, body language, and the like. Researchers must also determine whether it is necessary to transcribe verbal ticks (e.g., "ums," "you knows," dialect, and slang; see also Kowal & O'Connell, 2014, for a discussion about the importance of transcription techniques). In most cases, the more information that can be captured in the transcripts, the better. At the same time, researchers must consider whether reporting direct speech in research reports might embarrass the participant.

Whenever possible, it is helpful for interviewers to send a copy of the interview transcript to the participant for review, with the caveat that they might make changes to or clarify something they said over the course of the interview. This approach to member checking is a good tool for ensuring the trustworthiness of the data and for including participants more actively in the research process.

Gathering Field Notes and Observations

In addition to conducting interviews, observation is a powerful and common approach to qualitative data collection. According to Namey and Trotter (2015), "a strong participant observation design is a systematic and integrated multimethod approach to field-based data collection" (p. 449). Here, too, decisions about methods must logically connect to the guiding theory and objectives of the action research project. Observation can include a range of approaches, including "direct (in-context) observation" which includes "systematic—not impressionistic—recording of observational data," participation by the researcher "in order to gain both an empirical and humanistic understanding," and the "systematic collection of sociocultural narratives" (p. 449).

Since action researchers cannot be separated from the action, observation most often will include personal, impressionistic perceptions about the event being observed. McNiff and Whitehead (2010) describe the complex nature of observation in action research:

> In action research, you aim to observe yourself, in company with others, to see whether you are exercising your educational influence in their thinking, and they in yours. It is a reciprocal relationship, learning with and from one another. You are at the centre of the action, so this involves considerable honesty. (p. 157)

Unlike other forms of qualitative research, in action research the researcher is both the researcher and the researched. Observing one's own practice necessarily includes observing others' reactions to your practice as well as recording the action. For those interested in gaining outside perspectives, action researchers can invite colleagues to observe and record **field notes**. For example, a teacher may ask a colleague to observe her lesson and record field notes or an administrator may ask a colleague to observe her lead a meeting.

Planning for Observations

As in all forms of data collection, the purpose of observational inquiry is to understand a particular topic or phenomenon. To ensure that adequate data will be collected, action researchers must prepare for data collection. According to McNiff and Whitehead (2010), "before gathering data, be as clear as possible about what you are looking for, otherwise you may waste a lot of time" (p. 154). This involves creating a plan for observing, developing an observation protocol, and creating a system for recording field notes. Observations and field notes are most often associated with ethnographic approaches to qualitative inquiry. Just as anthropologists might seek to observe events to gain sociocultural understanding, so too action researchers may seek to collect data about events as they occur in real time. By recording field notes, the researcher can return to these notes later to analyze patterns. Planning for observations then includes not only selecting the time and place to observe but also preparing to gather observational field notes. Researchers should also set aside time immediately following the observation to expand on field notes and/or type field notes into transcriptions for later data analysis.

Developing Observation Protocols

Whereas ethnographers might prefer to collect open-ended, unscripted observation field notes, some researchers prefer to create protocols to guide observations. Doing so may help to ensure that the observer remains focused during the interview, for instance, remaining attuned to the topic under study and not getting distracted with the myriad actions and conversations that might occur in a public space. The relative open-endedness or tightness of the observation protocol will be related to the aim of the inquiry and the perspective of the researcher. Many action researchers in school settings will be familiar with tighter observation protocols, for instance, rubrics used by administrators to evaluate teaching. These can be retooled and adapted for the needs of individual action researchers to provide a source of data to be analyzed and compared.

Action Researcher Journal

Since action researchers interested in observing their own practice will not have the luxury of scripting field notes while they are teaching, keeping an action research journal can be a useful tool for data collection. The action researcher should plan to systematically record events, experiences, and reflections in the action research journal continuously throughout the project. Depending on the time and space available for journaling, action researchers may choose from a variety of strategies for keeping an action research journal. These range from jotting down notes to producing more formal research memos about data collection activities.

McNiff and Whitehead (2010) outline several possible uses of a research journal or "diary," including to keep a timeline of key events "to illustrate general points" through "'thick' descriptions that show the complexities of a situation," "to chart the progress of your action research," and as "a way of interrogating your own thinking" (p. 156). Action researchers may find that keeping a research journal not only provides a space to monitor the progress of the project but also the "process of reflective writing is an integral part of your professional development" (Koshy, 2010, p. 91). They can also ask participants (students, colleagues) to regularly record their thoughts or experiences in their own diaries. These diaries may later be used as part of the data analysis process if participants consent.

Memos

The research journal can provide a place to record events and to monitor one's interpretation of those events in the form of analytical **memos**. According to Corbin and Strauss (2015), "writing memos and doing diagrams often makes biases and assumptions obvious to the researcher" (p. 119). They are different than field notes in that "they are usually written after a researcher leaves the data-gathering site" and "they [memos] are more complex and analytical" (p. 120). Early in the research project memos may begin as rather short or benign documents. As time progresses and the action researcher has a better understanding of the project, they may evolve to be more complex and analytical. Memos provide a place to begin to make connections across data collection incidents and to interpret the meaning of the data collected. Eventually memos become their own form of data and should be treated as such. Be sure to carefully label, organize, and store memos for future reference and analysis. For example,

Schatzman and Strauss (1973) developed a strategy for noting "observational notes" (as ONs) separately from "theoretical notes" (TNs) and "methodological notes" (MNs; pp. 99–101). Researchers may also develop a system for when to record memos. In addition to creating memos after data collection, Corbin and Strauss (2015) recommend that researchers periodically create "summary memos" to "pull together all the information a researcher has on a concept and to get a sense of how major concepts might fit together" (p. 122). Memoing provides yet another example of the iterative nature of data collection and analysis. For action researchers, data analysis can be part of data collection, and analytical insights should be recorded in memos before they are lost (Patton, 2015).

Document Analysis and Unobtrusive Approaches to Data Collection

Once action researchers begin to approach their everyday practice as opportunities for data collection, data will appear more and more readily. The everyday artifacts created by practice, including documents, work outputs, and visual texts, provide evidence for later analysis. Even room arrangements and decorations become data "texts" to be read and analyzed. By analyzing the everyday ephemera of practice, action researchers can engage in unobtrusive approaches to data collection that yield important information about the contexts of practice as well as outcomes.

Documentary Artifacts

Perhaps the most common approach to unobtrusive data collection is to gather documents and artifacts related to practice. Of course, the way in which documents are collected and analyzed depends on the scope and aim of the guiding research question(s). Action researchers can use documents to provide context about data collection events, for instance, to understand the culture, tone, and values of an environment such as a classroom or a school. At the same time, documents can provide important information about practice. According to Koshy (2010), "documentary evidence can provide insights into a situation where research takes place" and can be gathered often with very little effort (p. 90). Documentary evidence or artifacts might include curriculum materials, textbooks, lesson plans, student handouts, text written on the board (e.g., learning objectives, assignments), and multimedia presentations. This form of data provides rich contextual information that may be explored more thoroughly through interviews or other approaches to data collection.

Student Work

Another relevant source of data for teacher action researchers is student work. This involves going beyond typical assessments (e.g., assigning grades) to look for patterns in student work and to compare and contrast across samples of student work. Obviously teachers can learn a great deal about student learning outcomes from the work students submit. They can also uncover misconceptions in student thinking and areas in need of additional teaching. Student work can be a great resource for prompting a think-aloud interview protocol with students. By going over work submitted one on one with a student, the teacher researcher can begin to better understand student thinking, motivation, and understanding that contributed to the work. This, in turn, can launch changes in instruction or reteaching.

Teacher Work Samples

Similar to student work samples, teacher work samples can provide more information about teacher practice and the decision-making processes that contribute to enacted curriculum in the classroom. Teacher work samples can include lesson plans or other artifacts of teaching practice. Teacher action researchers interested in studying their own practice may wish to keep annotated samples of their work to keep a record of their day-to-day decision-making as well as reflections about various aspects of a lesson or teaching activity. (See the activities section at the end of this chapter for an example activity and template.)

Action researchers can also build on the work of a consortium of teacher preparation institutions that have developed a systematic protocol for submitting teacher work samples. The guides for developing work samples as well as rubrics for assessing these samples are available through the Renaissance Teacher Work Samples home page (see http://www.wku.edu/rtwsc/). Action research collaboratives, including school-based action research networks, may find it useful to adapt these materials into a common format and rubric for use across multiple teacher action researchers. Establishing a common framework and approach to collecting teacher work samples will streamline the process of comparing across samples during the data analysis phase.

Visual Approaches to Data Collection

Visual images and representations can be valuable sources of information for action researchers. These data may provide sociocultural information about the context in which the research occurs. Researchers can use visual images as evidence or data or as part of their methods for developing a deeper understanding about the experiences of participants.

Visual approaches can be merged with other approaches to data collection, including interviews and observation. For example, one strategy for eliciting students to describe their experiences, understandings, and/or impressions is to have them draw a picture or find a representative image or object. The action researcher can then prompt students to describe the significance of the object or image in framing their thinking and understanding. In the process, the action researcher can gain a better understanding of student thinking.

One strategy for engaging participants in visual approaches to data collection is to ask them to locate images that serve as metaphors or visual representations of their experiences. For example, a student might choose a picture of a mountain to represent the challenge of reading nonfiction texts or a student might choose a picture of a heart to represent the importance of relationships in the classroom. Another approach is to provide the participants with a set of pictures or images and to ask them to organize the images in a system that makes sense to them. For the action researcher, visual approaches to data collection provide ready examples to compare and contrast across the participants. They also tend to "reveal underlying values or cognitive processes that verbal questioning might not reach" (Namey & Trotter, 2015, p. 465). Visual images may also serve as powerful examples to use in the final written report or presentation to summarize major findings.

Photovoice

Photovoice is a much more formalized approach to asking participants to represent their thinking through a combination of images and audio or text-based reflection. Considered a methodology in its own right, photovoice has been used in a variety of participatory action research studies to engage participants as co-researchers in community-based action research (see Blackman & Fairey, 2007). Here, participants are asked to take photographs related to the topic of study over a period of time. They are then asked to share their photos and discuss their meaning. According to Namey and Trotter (2015), photovoice can be used "to allow research participants to present a visual view of their world and then explain it" and "to collect compelling firsthand accounts" (p. 466).

Digital Storytelling

Similar to photovoice, digital storytelling provides a process for collecting data. Action researchers can ask participants to create digital stories to describe personal experiences as well as conceptual understandings. Digital stories are short (often 2–5 minutes) multimedia presentations. Students can use PowerPoint or video editing/producing tools such as iMovie or Microsoft Movie Maker to produce digital stories. An important characteristic of digital storytelling is the melding of images and narration. Student voice is a central aspect of digital storytelling that action researchers can mine for greater understanding of student experiences and student outcomes. Digital storytelling can also be used by the action researcher at the culmination of an action research project to summarize findings and discuss the importance of the findings (see also Chapter 7).

Triangulating Data Collection

It should be obvious by now that once the analytic mind is turned on, for action researchers data are everywhere. By using a variety of approaches to qualitative data collection, including interviews, observations, and artifacts, action researchers gather evidence to provide a "thick description" of an issue or topic of importance under study. By triangulating data collection—a process of collecting two or more types of data over multiple interactions—action researchers also enhance the credibility and trustworthiness of their findings and final research reports. Ultimately, the aim is to collect enough data or evidence to develop a clear understanding about an issue related to practice and to bring about change or improvement. Without sufficient data, from a variety of vantage points and perspectives, action researchers cannot make the informed decisions necessary to improve practice and bring about change. In the next chapter we will move from data collection toward data analysis, exploring analytical strategies for making sense of the data collected over the course of an action research project.

CHAPTER SUMMARY

- There are three main approaches to qualitative data collection: interview, observation, and document analysis.

- Interviews can be conducted one-on-one or in small focus groups. Interviews are rich sources of data that provide the opportunity to learn more about individual experiences in ways not afforded by other data collection techniques.

- Action researchers should consider the relative benefits of conducting one-on-one interviews or focus groups in advance of their data collection. Regardless of which approach

is taken, an interview protocol should be developed.

- Observation can be a useful tool for monitoring practice and the outcomes of participants. Action researchers may invite colleagues to observe their practice and take field notes or take notes during practice or in a researcher journal as a way to observe one's own practice.

- There are also many unobtrusive approaches to qualitative data collection such as document analysis and visual approaches, including digital storytelling and photovoice.

SUGGESTED WEB-BASED RESOURCES

Educational Uses of Digital Storytelling

http://digitalstorytelling.coe.uh.edu/index.cfm

"Four Rules of Active Listening"

https://www.state.gov/m/a/os/65759.htm

Introduction to Qualitative Interviews from the UK Data Service

https://www.ukdataservice.ac.uk/teaching-resources/interview/qualitative

Interviewing, from the Robert Wood Johnson Foundation's Qualitative Research Guidelines Project

http://www.qualres.org/HomeInte-3595.html

Observation, from the Robert Wood Johnson Foundation's Qualitative Research Guidelines Project

http://www.qualres.org/HomeObse-3594.html

FHI's Participant Observation from Qualitative Research Methods: A Data Collector's Field Guide

https://www.fhi360.org/resource/qualitative-research-methods-data-collectors-field-guide

Photovoice

https://photovoice.org/

StoryCenter

https://www.storycenter.org/about/

Strategies for Qualitative Interviews

http://sociology.fas.harvard.edu/files/sociology/files/interview_strategies.pdf

QUESTIONS AND ACTIVITIES

Reflection Questions

1. Based on what you read, what are the most logical approaches to qualitative data collection that you can use to study your practice and answer your research question(s)?

2. What are some ways that you can integrate qualitative data collection into your daily practice?

3. Who can help you with your data collection? Are there any colleagues that you can collaborate with or ask to help?

Practice Activities

Activity 5A: Developing a Plan for Data Collection

In this activity, you will focus on identifying and planning your data collection strategies. Two overarching questions guide this activity:

- What are the strategies that can be used in action research to collect data?

- Which of these do you plan to include in your research proposal?

On a separate page, briefly complete each of the following:

1. Clearly identify the research question(s) that will guide your study.

2. Describe the context of your study: Where will the study take place? Who will be involved in the study? What is important background information for understanding the setting, group of participants, and/or issue being addressed in your study?

3. Describe the data collection methods: Where will the data be collected? How long will the data be collected, including number of events and duration? Who will be engaged in the data collection process?

After you have finished drafting this discussion of your methods, keep it handy as you proceed through your action research study. This section can also easily be developed into paragraphs to form the basis of your methodology section in a future written report about your action research study.

Activity 5B: Developing an Interview Protocol

Follow these steps for developing a semistructured interview protocol.

1. Begin by reviewing your research question(s) and the purpose and need for your study. Reflect on potential affordances of using interview questions to help you answer your research questions and ultimately to address a problem associated with practice.

2. Identify a sample of participants and make plans for recruiting these participants.

3. Draft a series of three to five semistructured interview questions that you plan to ask participants. Be sure to double-check that the questions align with the research questions.

4. Add an additional opening question to your protocol that is designed to build rapport and provide the participants with an opportunity to introduce themselves.

5. Add an additional open-ended question to the end of your interview protocol. This question should be designed to prompt participants to add any additional information they might deem relevant. For example, you might ask, "Is there anything that you wish I had asked? Or is there anything else I should know?"

Activity 5C: Practicing Your Interviewing Skills

Although our culture is steeped in interviewing, it can be difficult to conduct effective research interviews. After reviewing the discussion of strategies for successful interviews, select a time for practicing your skills. Follow these steps:

1. Choose an interview partner. This person can be a colleague or friend. This activity works best if you do not choose a family member or close friend, since the aim is to mimic interviewing someone that you want to learn more about.

2. Develop a short list of questions related to a fairly mundane topic (e.g., "How do you like to spend your leisure time?" or "Describe your typical day.").

3. As you engage in your interview, practice your active listening skills. Be sure to pose follow-up and probing questions, designed to get a better understanding of the participant's experiences. If you are able to, audio record the interview.

4. Reflect on the interview process. If you recorded the interview, monitor your interactions with the speaker. Did you interrupt? Did you probe effectively? Were there places where you could have asked more or talked less?

Note: An alternative is to test your interview protocol with a small sample of participants and then refine your questions based on your results.

Activity 5D: Developing Skills of Observation

Similar to conducting interviews, gathering data through observation is a skill that can be developed over time. Perhaps most important is to develop the skill of remaining focused on the purpose of the observation, rather than being distracted by ancillary activity occurring at the site of data collection. For this activity, follow these steps:

1. Select a site for observation. This could be a public space or a more directed environment, such as a classroom, where you can remain a fairly passive participant observer (i.e., not directly contributing to the action).

2. Prior to the observation, divide a paper into two columns. (You can use pen/pencil or your computer. Use the following format:

Your name:

Date/time:

Name of location:

	(Begin typing or writing here. Once you have completed your observation, you may decide to go back and add numbers to each line.)

3. Record field notes in the right-hand column only. As you observe you might divide the time into 5-minute increments to try out various approaches to observation.

   a. Jotting: developing a shorthand approach to recording all observed action as accurately as possible

   b. Tallying: creating a table or chart to tally the number of times an action occurs or is observed (e.g., students answering questions, student time on task)

   c. Timed observation: focus on one aspect of the space or action to record via field notes for a set amount of time. Once the time is up, move onto another aspect or action.

4. Optional: Add a map of the space and experiment with various strategies for monitoring action within the space (e.g., numbering observed participants, tallying participant actions, drawing arrows to demarcate action).

5. We will return to this activity in the next chapter, where you will add codes to the left-hand column for each line or groups of text in the right-hand column.

6. Reflect on the process. What went well? What was difficult about the observation process? As you look over your transcript, what information seems to be missing or still needed?

   Note: An alternative is to view a video of an educational setting via YouTube or some other web-based, video sharing tool.

Activity 5E: Research Plan

Returning to Activity 4B from Chapter 4, revise your research plan.

1. After further reflection, what aspect of your practice are you interested in studying? What is the guiding question(s) for your research project?

2. Why are you interested in studying this part of your practice? What significance/importance does it hold in your work? Explain.

3. What relevant literature or outside resources will inform your project?

4. What have you learned so far from working on your study?

5. How are you going to collect data now? Or describe your current process of data collection.

6. Why this method of data collection?

7. How will you protect your participants? (Ethics documentation)

8. How might you analyze your data?

9. When can you collect and analyze your data?

10. How will you involve your students, colleagues, peers, and others in your study? Who can help you with your research project?

SHORTCUTS FOR QUALITATIVE DATA COLLECTION IN ACTION RESEARCH OR MINI-STUDY

Not every teacher has the time or opportunity to conduct a thorough action research study. This should not prohibit teachers from pursuing their own systematic and intentional inquiry in their classrooms. There are many ways to adapt the research cycle to meet individual needs and constraints. Below are suggestions for conducting shortened forms of qualitative data collection to inform practice.

Keep a Journal

All teachers can benefit from reflection on practice. By keeping a daily or weekly journal, teachers can record teaching activities and strategies. They can also make notes to track student progress and their own impressions about daily classroom life. Over time, the journal will provide a useful tool for monitoring progress and working for change. Teachers can refer to the journal for future planning and as evidence of their own professional growth. Those seeking greater organization may choose to follow a protocol or template that includes all of the following information:

• Date

• Topic(s) taught

• Strategies used

• Student outcomes

• What went well

• What should be changed in future classes

Conduct Short Interviews With Students

Although teachers work closely with students every day, they rarely have focused opportunities to get to know their students and to understand their experiences. By conducting short (5 minutes or less) interviews with students throughout the school year, teachers can create a systematic approach to monitoring student outcomes and experiences, while gaining valuable insight about their own practice. Interviewing students also provides students with a "voice" in the classroom and may help to build trust as students realize the teacher cares about their ideas.

Just as you would in a longer, more traditional interview, first consider the information you hope to gain from the interview. For example, are you hoping to develop trust and relationships? Or are you interested in learning your students' impressions about your most recent lesson or how they feel about math or other subjects? Once you frame your purposes, you can jot down short, open-ended questions to guide the interview. You may choose to conduct the interviews when students arrive to school early, complete their work, during centers, at the end of the day, or during other periods of downtime.

An even shorter version of conducting interviews is to provide students with an opportunity to provide written feedback, perhaps via a student course evaluation that the teacher creates, a suggestion box, or through a modified version of the Twitter hashtag #wishmyteacherknew (see also http://iwishmyteacherknewbook.com/).

Analyze Student Work

Teachers often approach student work from a focus on assessment (e.g., grading for incorrect responses). However, teachers can borrow from the philosophy of action research to view student work as a diagnostic tool. For example, by analyzing a single student's work over time, a teacher can identify patterns and misconceptions. Similarly, by examining student work across an entire class, a teacher might identify areas that need to be retaught. In some cases, teachers may discover through their analysis that the assessments themselves need to be revised to more clearly capture student understanding. Some questions may be misleading or confusing to students and not really garner the kind of information teachers need to

assess student understanding about a topic or content area.

Lesson Study

In some instances, teachers may choose to focus on a single day's lesson or unit for improvement. Here, they may find it helpful to invite outside observers into their classroom to take field notes. Since teaching a new topic or using new strategies is often all-consuming, an extra set of eyes in the classroom may provide much-needed feedback about the effectiveness of the lesson, including the clarity of ideas being discussed and student experiences. The same could perhaps be done by video recording the lesson, but there may be added benefit from having an opportunity to debrief with a colleague. Perhaps you could identify a partner to trade off duties of teaching and observing. It is important to note that both the teacher being observed and the teacher who is observing may benefit from this close-up lesson study.

CHAPTER 6

Understanding Through Qualitative Data Analysis

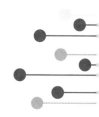

Guiding Questions

1. What is the aim of qualitative data analysis for action researchers?
2. What are procedures to follow to analyze qualitative data collected during action research?
3. How can action researchers ensure that their data analysis is trustworthy?

Keywords and Glossary

Attribute coding: is highlighting/noting the basic information of the transcript, including setting, context, and participant demographics. Also a data management approach.

Axial coding: is conducted after the initial coding of data is completed when researchers compare and contrast across codes to identify points of intersection or difference.

Code: is a word, short phrase, or symbol used to describe an aspect of the data collected and to reduce data into manageable pieces.

Constant comparative methods: include comparing and contrasting across data and the codes assigned to data.

Critical friend: acts as a sounding board throughout the research process to provide feedback and review the work of action researchers.

Descriptive coding: involves summarizing the basic topic of a line or lines of data in a transcript of data.

Inductive approach: is an open-ended approach to developing assertions about data, based on the data themselves.

In vivo coding: is coding a line(s) of the transcript using words or phrases found in the transcript.

Member check: refers to the process of engaging research participants in checking the data and data analysis to ensure that the researcher has drawn accurate conclusions based on the data.

Process coding: focuses on noting action found in transcripts using gerunds (*-ing* words).

QDAS: is the acronym for qualitative data analysis software. These computer-based tools can be used during data analysis to organize data and refine codes and categories.

Structural coding: uses a set of codes developed prior to the research study based on the research question or review of the literature and assigns these codes to a line(s) of data.

Values coding: infers the values and beliefs of the participants as described through the transcripts of data.

Chapter Introduction

Because the aim of qualitative data collection is to capture a "thick description" of a problem under study, action researchers may feel overwhelmed by the great deal of data they collect over the course of their work. Data analysis is the process of making sense of those data and drawing lessons from the data in order to transform practice. According to Merriam (2009), "making sense out of data involves consolidating, reducing, and interpreting what people have said and what the researcher has seen and read—it is the process of making meaning" (pp. 175–176). Data analysis is both an art and a science; it is a process that involves both creativity and evidence. Namey and Trotter (2015) outline the following steps to guide qualitative data analysis:

- Reading/reviewing data with research/analysis objectives in mind
- Identifying key concepts, ideas, and themes in data
- Defining and codifying important ideas and themes in a codebook
- Coding data, preferably with two independent coders
- Summarizing coded data by
  - looking for patterns and relationships among themes;

- identifying theme frequencies to help identify the most salient ideas across data;
- using quantitative data reduction techniques as appropriate; and
- referring back to qualitative data, using quotes to emphasize findings (p. 468).

Data Analysis and Action Research

While there are common elements to qualitative data analysis, including coding data and looking for patterns across the data, it is important to keep in mind that action research is a unique form of inquiry. Since data are collected in situ, in the midst of practice, action researchers do not have the luxury of bracketing data analysis as a discrete step, nor should they. It makes sense that action researchers are constantly interpreting what they encounter over the course of data collection and using the data to inform their practice. For example, a teacher action researcher would not wish to ignore data collected from students to inform her teaching practices until she has taken the time to analyze it. Rather, insights about practice derived during practice must immediately take effect.

Returning to our action research cycle, we are reminded in Figure 6.1 that action researchers use analytical strategies across the five phases of the cycle, including problem posing, action, observation, reflection, and sharing. However, although we aim to view the action research cycle as an iterative, overlapping process, it is sometimes more manageable in practice for action researchers to pursue a linear process of data collection and analysis. This is particularly true for action researchers who are participating in courses or other professional learning opportunities with expectations for producing final research reports. The same may be true

Figure 6.1 The Action Research Cycle

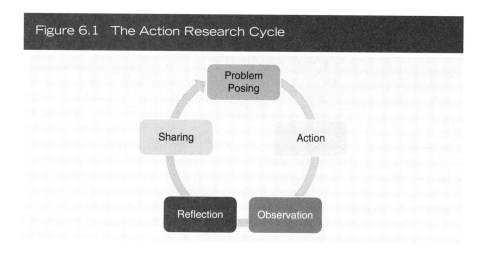

for action researchers who need to respond to particular audiences (e.g., administrators or policy makers). Following a cycle that resembles the typical process of educational research—question, action, data collection, analysis, and reporting—may be most familiar and expected. (See also the shortcuts at the end of this chapter.)

The main thrust of the action, observation, and reflection stages of the action research cycle will include data collection and analysis. In other words, here the action researcher is engaging in *action, observing* the impact of the action by collecting data and evidence from a variety of sources, and working to *reflect* on the meaning of data collected through inductive analysis. In the sections below, data analysis is described as a formal process used to summarize the data and lead to the development of logical assertions about what the data mean. The caveat here is that in many action research projects, data analysis will be ongoing and iterative; action researchers may return to their data multiple times for additional analysis.

Procedures for Data for Qualitative Analysis

This text will focus on open-ended, inductive approaches to coding. It will also refer to **constant comparative methods** to compare **codes** across data collected in the action research study and to identify emergent themes in the data or "grounded theory" (Glaser & Strauss, 1967). Below we will describe the process of moving from initial coding strategies toward categorization and, ultimately, developing preliminary findings and assertions.

Preparing Data for Analysis

Preparing data for analysis will follow directly from the procedures for data collection (see Activity 6A: Creating a Data Analysis Plan). As mentioned previously, action researchers need to have a system in place for labeling and storing data. This system should include noting information about the date, setting, and area of focus for the data collection event. It is also important for action researchers to monitor the quality of data throughout their work to ensure they are collecting data that respond to the research objectives. A good rule of thumb to keep your research question(s) central to your data collection and analysis is to jot down the research question on a sticky note or on a whiteboard near the computer. Add your research questions to the top of data collection protocols and transcripts to help maintain the research focus. Once transcripts of the data are created, you are ready to begin the data analysis process by coding lines or segments of data.

Coding Qualitative Data

Most action researchers who embrace an interpretivist perspective use an open-ended, **inductive approach** to analyzing data. Using what is sometimes referred to as a grounded theory approach (Corbin & Strauss, 2008; Glaser & Strauss, 1967), researchers identify codes, categories, and patterns within the data to develop assertions about the topic under study. According to Saldaña (2016), "a code in qualitative inquiry is most often a word or short phrase that symbolically assigns a summative, salient, essence-capturing, and/or evocative attribute for a portion of language-based or visual data" (p. 4). Through coding, researchers ascribe symbolic meaning to bits of data. In some cases, researchers will use preexisting theoretical models to describe the data or develop new theories based on their analysis. The inductive method assumes generalizations about the data will "bubble" up from the data.

Action researchers should begin data analysis by immersing themselves in their data. This involves reading and rereading transcripts of data collected over the course of the study. Since action research is about practice, action researchers must also be able to contend with the tension between intimately knowing the context of the data, while also being able to analytically and critically reflect on the data. Added to the burden on the researcher is the sheer volume of data that is often collected over the course of study. It can feel overwhelming for action researchers to prepare to make sense of the multitude of data collected. It is important, therefore, for action researchers to have a plan in place for data analysis and to use analytical coding techniques to make sense of the data by chunking it down into pieces.

Put simply, coding qualitative data is the process of reducing data into manageable pieces. It begins with reading through transcriptions of data and jotting notes in the margins. "This process of making notations next to bits of data that strike you as potentially relevant for answering your research questions is also called *coding*" (Merriam, 2009, p. 178). Through a process of coding—identifying pieces of data based on their most salient characteristics—the action researcher begins to make sense of what the data mean. You can think of coding data as similar to sorting groceries in a shopping cart (Merriam, 2009, p. 177). As you remove pieces of food from the cart, you almost imperceptibly, but purposely, assign them a descriptor (e.g., "fruit," "meat," "dairy," "veggie"). As you continue to sort, you make or refine your codes or descriptors (e.g., "citrus fruit," "green veggies," "healthy food," "junk food"). Similarly, action researchers, rather than report data verbatim, must make sense of the data collected. This is done by organizing and analyzing data to determine the relevance for improving practice. According to Henning, Stone, and Kelly (2009), researchers develop coding schemes by looking for "themes (consistent ideas which emerged), incidence (when and where something occurred) and trends (the frequency of patterns) (Macintyre, 2000)" (p. 103).

Once action researchers have returned to their data and read through the transcripts, they are ready to code. A good place to begin is with the researcher memos and researcher journal described in Chapter 4. Since these two sources of information recorded not only data but also initial analytical thoughts, they can be important resources for embarking on data analysis. By reading through these sources of data, the action researcher can develop an initial coding scheme. Codes can also be derived from the review of the literature, "theory-generated codes" (see Saldaña, 2016), or from the data collection files themselves, "in vivo" (using word and phases gathered through data collection) and inductive codes (see Marshall & Rossman, 2016, and Activity 6B: Practice Coding an Interview Transcript).

Approaches to Coding

There are many approaches to coding qualitative data. Determining which coding method is most appropriate depends on the purpose of the study, including the research questions, as well as the theoretical framework. For novice researchers, it might be helpful to begin working through Saldaña's (2016) "'generic' coding methods," which include "attribute coding," "structural coding or holistic coding," "descriptive coding," and "in vivo coding, process coding, and/or values coding" (p. 73). These approaches are described in more detail below and are offered as suggestions to provide structure to the data analysis process. After exploring these approaches to coding data, action researchers are encouraged to select a few to guide their own analysis. By planning in advance, the process of data analysis is more manageable and organized. At the end of the section, Table 6.1 describes suggested steps in using these coding strategies (see also Activity 6C: Practicing Data Analysis With Your Data).

Attribute Coding. Through **attribute coding**, the researcher notes "basic descriptive information" about the setting, participant demographics, or other key characteristics of the data. According to Saldaña (2016), "attribute coding is good qualitative data management and provides essential participant information and contexts for analysis and interpretation" (p. 83). This first-glance approach to coding the data also provides the researcher with an opportunity to audit the data and to identify what has been collected and what may be missing.

Structural Coding. **Structural coding** involves a process of applying "a content-based or conceptual phrase representing a topic of inquiry to a segment of data" (Saldaña, 2016, p. 98). In other words, these codes are developed prior to analysis and based on the topic of study. This approach might be particularly well suited to interview transcripts and open-ended survey results. The aim here is to create a coding system based on the research or interview questions to enable categorization of the data and easy comparison across the data. This process might involve coding segments of interview transcripts in which participants are asked the same question. Then these segments can be "pulled out" of the data and compared to identify patterns or themes. For example, if a teacher asks her students to respond to an interview question about her approach to teaching mathematics in cooperative groups, she could readily compare across the responses to identify potential themes.

Holistic Coding. Whereas structural coding may follow an inquiry-based approach to analysis, holistic coding begins with a big-picture look at the data that have been collected. In this way, holistic coding is different from structural coding in that it seeks to take a macro-level approach to coding data. In other words, the researcher aims "to grasp basic themes or issues in the data by absorbing them as a whole rather than by analyzing them line by line" (Dey, 1993, p. 104). This method may be most suitable to novice researchers or those engaged in more exploratory study. In order to engage in effective holistic coding, the researcher will need to have some sense about the direction of the analysis and be able to "'chunk' the text into broad topics" (Saldaña, 2016, p. 166). For example, an action researcher might code an entire research journal entry with a single theme (e.g., "student resistance" or "aha moment"). Holistic coding is probably a good first step toward more detailed coding that will come later since it involves the process of taking a broad view of portions of data.

Descriptive Coding **Descriptive coding**, also called topic coding, "summarizes in a word or short phrase—most often a noun—the basic topic of a passage of qualitative data" (Saldaña, 2016, p. 102). Unlike other "meaning-driven methods" of coding, this approach assigns basic descriptive terms to pieces of data to describe what is happening (Wolcott, 1994). This process might be particularly helpful for longitudinal studies to understand change over time. However, in vivo coding, process coding, and/or values coding may be more suitable for smaller-scale studies or case studies (Saldaña, 2016).

In Vivo Coding In vivo coding may be one of the most familiar and commonly used approaches to coding qualitative data (see also Charmaz, 2014; Corbin & Strauss, 2015). **In vivo coding** "refers to a word or short phrase from the actual language found in the qualitative data record" (Saldaña, 2016, p. 105) or "the terms used by participants themselves" (Strauss, 1987, p. 33). The researcher develops codes based on the information found verbatim in the data transcripts. This is a practical approach for action researchers in particular since it ensures that the researcher draws on the words of the participants and is "more likely to capture the meanings inherent in people's experiences" (Stringer, 2014, p. 140). For example, as a researcher begins to analyze transcripts from interviews, she may highlight or underline phrases spoken by the participant(s) that seem to be particularly relevant or salient to answering the research question. These words or phrases can become codes. Saldaña (2016) recommends that researchers use quotation marks to note in vivo codes that are derived from the participants.

Process Coding **Process coding**, or action coding, is used to "connote action in the data" (Saldaña, 2016, p. 111). According to Corbin and Strauss (2015), "the processes of human action can be strategic, routine, random, novel, automatic, and/or thoughtful" (p. 283). Since process codes focus on action, they are often gerunds (words ending in -*ing*, such as "reading," "watching," "learning," or "smiling"). This approach to coding can and should be used with other approaches to coding and may be most suitable to studies that focus on processes and routines (Saldaña, 2016). According to Charmaz (2008), "when you have studied a process, your categories will reflect its phases" (p. 106). As a result of process coding, researchers may be able to develop insights about the stages or series of steps that occur to contribute to action. These steps may be displayed in a visual diagram or in a series of bullet points or numbered items (see also Corbin & Strauss, 2015).

Values Coding. "**Values coding** is the application of codes to qualitative data that reflect a participant's values, attitudes, and beliefs, representing his or her perspectives or worldview" (Saldaña, 2016, p. 131). Whereas Saldaña differentiates between codes that refer to "values," "attitudes," or "beliefs," a researcher may choose not to deal with such nuance. Rather, it might suffice to simply code to identify participant beliefs and perspectives. It is important to note that compared to other more direct approaches to coding data, here the researcher is ascribing their own perspective about the other's beliefs. It is very important then that researchers gain a variety of types of data on which to build these assertions as well as to check in with participants. For example, whereas participants may cue researchers to things they value (e.g., "I really enjoy" or "I like"), it may be more helpful for researchers to probe directly for understanding about that which participants value (e.g., "What do you value?"; see Saldaña, 2016, p. 134).

Regardless of the approach taken, the action researcher can choose to code transcripts of data line by line or by lumping lines of text together (see Saldaña's, 2016, discussion of "lumping" and "splitting" data, pp. 23–25). Often researchers will develop some form of shorthand for noting codes directly on the transcripts. This might include using abbreviations, color schemes, numerical notations, or short phrases. As an example, Table 6.1 provides suggested steps for using the coding methods described above. You can find an example of how these coding approaches might be applied to a transcript of a focus group interview in the appendix of this chapter.

Approaches to coding are often very individualistic and it may take novice researchers some time to develop an approach to coding that feels comfortable and fruitful. Eventually, the aim is to group codes together according to themes to refine initial codes as the data analysis process progresses—a process referred to as "axial coding" (Corbin & Strauss, 2008).

Axial Coding and the Constant Comparative Method

After action researchers complete their initial coding of data, they move on to axial coding. Here, action researchers consider the differences and similarities among codes assigned to pieces of data or evidence. According to Marshall and Rossman (2016), "the codes are clustered around points of intersection, or axes," and result from "complex thinking that is a mix of induction and deduction—working back and forth from the emerging 'grounded theory' to specific clusters of data, back to the emerging theory with modifications, and so on" (p. 223). In other words, the researcher engages in a process of refining the language ascribed to observed phenomena to account for important nuances that appear in the data.

Table 6.1	Suggested Steps for Initial Coding Approaches	
Coding Approach	**Description**	**Duration**
Step 1: Attribute coding	Highlight/note the basic information of the transcript, including setting, context, participant demographics.	Simple, short
Step 2: Descriptive coding	Summarize the basic topic of a line or lines of data in the transcript. Can choose from four approaches here or use a combination of approaches: 2A: Structural coding—prior to data analysis, develop a set of codes based on the research question or review of the literature and assign these codes to a line(s) of data. 2B: In vivo—code a line(s) of the transcript using words or phrases found in the transcript. 2C: Process coding—note action found in transcripts using gerunds (-*ing* words). 2D: Values coding—infer the values and beliefs of the participants as described through the transcripts and make note of these as codes for a line(s) of the transcript.	Extensive, comprehensive
Step 3: Holistic coding	Assign either an entire piece of data or larger chunk of data with a macro-level code to describe it.	Macro-level review, short

In order to group and refine initial codes, action researchers must compare across data sources. This will necessitate going beyond memos and researcher journal entries to include other data collected over the course of the study (e.g., interview, observation, and document based). According to Corbin and Strauss (2015), a constant comparative method of data analysis is "the analytic process of comparing different pieces of data against each other for similarities and differences" (p. 85). This method of analysis seeks to make sense of the range of data collected as well as the various types of data collected. In Chapter 5, we discussed the importance of triangulating data collection to increase the trustworthiness of findings. Constantly comparing across the data—monitoring codes across various sources of data— leverages the range of data collected across the study. By determining whether data are conceptually similar, the action researcher can begin to derive meaning from the data. Areas of conceptual similarity and difference become important for understanding patterns and developing categories to describe the data.

Developing Categories

Through the process of constantly comparing across codes, action researchers move toward developing more abstract categories to describe the data collected. According to Marshall and Rossman (2016), "the tough intellectual work of analysis is generating categories and themes" (p. 220). Here, the action researcher goes beyond description toward interpretation and explanation (McNiff & Whitehead,

2010). Miles, Huberman, and Saldaña (2014) describe the process of data analysis as moving toward increasingly abstract concepts and theories: from data, to codes; to categories, themes, and concepts; and, ultimately, to assertions and theory. Here, the constant comparative method involves looking across codes to develop categories. The process of moving from coding to categorization and eventually to developing theories about the topic under study involves continually refining the way in which the data are described and named. The researcher is looking for patterns, "repetitive, regular, or consistent occurrences of action/data that appear more than twice" (Saldaña, 2016, p. 5). Once data have been coded, action researchers compare across codes to develop larger, overarching categories.

Assigning categories to sets of coded data might be imagined as being similar to putting data together in defined baskets or buckets. Returning to the previous shopping cart metaphor, here you group together all of the things you labeled as fruits into a single bin or basket, veggies into another basket. You might further group items from the cart based on other concrete categories: "dry goods" or "refrigerated items" or more subjective categories, such as "healthy foods" or "junk foods." Qualitative data analysis parallels our natural tendency to create conceptual frameworks to make sense of the things we observe in everyday life.

Diagramming Data Analysis

As data are being analyzed, action researchers can look across codes and categories assigned to data to create visual diagrams. According to Corbin and Strauss (2015), "Diagrams are conceptual visualizations of data, and because they are conceptual, diagrams help to raise the researcher's thinking beyond the level of description" (p. 122). Not only do diagrams enable action researchers to organize and arrange data, they also can help researchers identify concepts within the data and relationships across the data. Diagrams may be very simple or more complex; regardless, they force researchers to "think about the data in 'lean ways'" (p. 123). By creating a visual image or map of data analysis, diagrams help action researchers identify relationships between concepts found in the data (see Activity 6D: Developing a Visual Diagram of Your Data).

Seeking Emergent Themes and Theories of Practice

Through the process of coding data transcripts, comparing across data sources, and clustering codes together, either through written or visual analysis, action researchers can begin to develop emergent themes and findings. The conceptual frameworks that emerge from data analysis in action research can be described as "theories of practice." Through the process of consciously posing questions about practice and collecting and analyzing relevant data, action researchers begin to make explicit their previously held implicit or subconscious ideas, beliefs, or theories about practice. In the process of interrogating these theories of practice, action researchers develop and refine their practical theories—that is, theories that derive from the study of practice—a process that is likely to bring about change in practice. For example, according to Elliott (2007), "since practical theories have normative implications, one would expect these new theories to be reflected in conscious changes in teaching approach" (p. 50). In other words, through the process of identifying how things should change based on a comprehensive analysis of the data, the action researcher makes assertions about a particular course of action.

The Logistics of Data Analysis

Just as it is important for action researchers to develop systems for data collection, so too they must develop consistent systems for data analysis. In the section above, we created a rough outline for data analysis:

- Developing initial coding schemes through the process of coding transcripts

- Conducting axial coding through a constant comparative method

- Using diagrams to create visual representations of data

- Developing concepts from categories

- Seeking emergent themes and theories of practice

While these steps are designed to move the data analysis from the more concrete to more abstract, they also may make the process more manageable.

First, action researchers must develop a coding system that makes logical sense and can be returned to and refined over time. Researchers may want to create a "code book"—where they can create a list of codes and their meaning for future reference. As the researcher moves from initial coding toward categorization and conceptualization, it may be helpful to begin creating new documents to record and organize data. For example, you can create a folder on your computer and then add separate word-processing files/documents for each category. The name of each file could correspond to the category. In these files you can copy and paste representative pieces of data from the transcripts to refer to relevant codes and categories. Eventually you can layer in descriptive paragraphs—for instance, introducing the category—and merge these files later to develop the final report. Some researchers may choose an analog approach—printing out copies of transcripts to code and then literally cutting transcripts up and organizing them in piles. Action researchers may also find qualitative data analysis software useful for organizing data analysis.

Qualitative Data Analysis Software (QDAS)

Action researchers can upload copies of their data transcripts to **QDAS** for further analysis. It is important to note that QDAS will not analyze the data for you. Rather, the researcher must assign codes to pieces of data just as they would in analog approaches to data analysis. The benefit of QDAS is that it offers a way to organize large sets of qualitative data. It ensures the ready retrieval of data and enables the researcher to link pieces of data that are assigned similar codes. These programs also often offer ways to visually represent data. Currently there are several available software choices on the market, including Atlas.ti, NVivo, and Dedoose. In addition to these software packages, action researchers can also use Excel spreadsheets to assist in data analysis.

Understanding Validity and Trustworthiness

Action researchers are held to standards of validity and trustworthiness. This means action researchers must present sound and logical arguments to describe the conclusions they have made, based on the data collected. They are required to make the case to warrant their assertions. In addition to collecting multiple sources of data and engaging in multiple approaches to data analysis, there are specific strategies that action researchers can use to enhance the credibility of their projects. These include engaging critical friends as outside readers and discussants and sharing findings with participants through "member checks."

Engaging a Critical Friend

Throughout the action research process, it is invaluable to work with a **critical friend** (see Activity 6E: Critical Friend Check-In). This is someone who can be a sounding board throughout the process of problem posing, action, observation, reflection, and reporting. Particularly in regard to data analysis, critical friends can provide valuable feedback about the saliency of concepts derived from the data. They can review visual diagrams and coding schemes to provide feedback, ask questions, and prompt further analysis. In some cases, engaging different critical friends at different points in the process will be helpful. For example, when you are initiating your study it might be helpful to have a colleague or someone very familiar with your topic work with you. Later in the process it might be useful to share your findings with someone less familiar with the topic. Being able to clearly articulate your interpretations to various audiences will provide useful sources of feedback.

Member Check

In addition to engaging outsiders as critical friends in the action research, you may also engage participants to guide your analysis. Participants can conduct a "**member check**" about specific pieces of data or your interpretation of the data. For example, you might share an interview transcript with a participant to ask them for further information or to check if your transcription accurately captured their meaning. At the same time, you could share analytical memos, diagrams, and initial drafts of the final research report with participants to determine whether your interpretation matches theirs. In many cases, participants can often extend your initial analysis by offering their own perspectives or interpretations.

Reflection

Qualitative data analysis is a complex process that seems to be both an art and a science. For action researchers, this process is even more complicated given the intimate nature of the research. Action researchers must contend with looking inward, while also opening up to critical scrutiny. Through deliberate and systematic qualitative analysis and interpretation, action researchers can develop new understandings related to practice. These understandings can lead to new directions in practice and eventual change. As long as action researchers keep in mind the reasons why they collect data—to provide evidence, and "in order to provide evidence you need to analyse the data you have collected" (Koshy, 2010, p. 118)—perhaps the process of data analysis will feel less daunting and more directed. As a result of the data collected and analyzed, the action researcher generates new knowledge. The next step will be to "articulate the knowledge you have generated, how it has affected your practice and what significance it may have for other practitioners" (Koshy, 2010, p. 119). This will occur in the final reflection and writing portions of your project.

CHAPTER SUMMARY

- Qualitative data analysis can be daunting; however, with a plan and process in place, action researchers can make sense of the multitude of data collected over the course of a project.

- Action researchers can choose from a variety of approaches to data analysis and coding based on the research aims and research questions posed.

- After initial coding is conducted, action researchers move on to compare across codes and to develop categories.

- It may be helpful for action researchers to create a visual diagram of codes and categories to help make sense of the data collected and move toward the written report of the research.

- Action researchers are ethically bound to ensure that their data analysis and findings are trustworthy by collecting multiple sources of data, engaging in multiple approaches to data analysis, and using strategies such as engaging a critical friend and member checking.

SUGGESTED WEB-BASED RESOURCES

Analyzing Qualitative Data (from the Pell Institute)

http://toolkit.pellinstitute.org/evaluation-guide/analyze/analyze-qualitative-data/

Atlas.ti

http://atlasti.com/

Dedoose

http://www.dedoose.com/

How to Do Action Research in Your Classroom (Teachers Network Leadership Institute)

http://www.teachersnetwork.org/tnli/Action_Research_Booklet.pdf (See Chapter 3, "Making Sense of Experience" [p. 8] and "Analyzing Your Data" [p. 14])

NVivo

http://www.qsrinternational.com/nvivo-product

Our Action Research (Teachers Network Leadership Institute)

http://www.teachersnetwork.org/tnli/research/

Using Excel for Qualitative Data Analysis

http://www.betterevaluation.org/en/resources/guide/using_excel_for_qualitative_data_analysis

QUESTIONS AND ACTIVITIES

Reflection Questions

1. What are the different approaches to coding, and how might these approaches impact your analysis? Which of the approaches seems to be most effective for your work?

2. What are steps to follow in data analysis?

3. How can action researchers ensure the trustworthiness of their data analysis?

Practice Activities

Activity 6A: Creating a Data Analysis Plan

In this activity, you will focus on identifying and planning your data analysis strategies. Two overarching questions guide this activity:

- *What are the strategies that can be used in your action research project to analyze data?*

- *Which of these do you plan to include in your research proposal?*

On a separate page, briefly complete each of the following:

1. Restate the research question(s) that guide your study.

2. Create a list of the data collected over the course of the study using brief descriptions such as the type of data and context (e.g., interview on [insert date] about study strategies).

3. Next, create a timeline for data analysis.

   - Which data will you analyze and in what order?

- Which initial coding strategies will you use?
- At what point will you begin axial coding?
- What is your deadline for coding across the data and creating a visual diagram?
- What strategies will you use to improve the trustworthiness of your data analysis?

After you have finished drafting this description of your data analysis methods, keep it handy as you proceed through your analysis. This description can be used to describe your data analysis in a future written report about your action research study.

Activity 6B: Practice Coding an Interview Transcript

In the appendix, there is an example transcript from a focus group interview conducted with seventh graders. Analyze the transcript using a variety of the initial coding strategies described in this chapter. Next, review the annotated version of the transcript. Were there any similarities or differences in your analysis?

Activity 6C: Practicing Data Analysis With Your Data

Next, select a transcript of your own data. Work through the suggested steps for initial data analysis as described in the table below.

What worked for you?
What would you change in future data analysis?

Activity 6D: Developing a Visual Diagram of Your Data

After you have analyzed across several transcripts of your data and engaged in axial coding, begin to create a visual diagram of your data. This could be in the form of a concept map or diagram. The aim here is to create a visual picture of your analysis with representative pieces of data.

Activity 6E: Critical Friend Check-In

Identify a colleague or peer who can work with you as a critical friend. Arrange a time to meet with the friend to discuss your action research project. Prior to the meeting, take a few moments

Coding Approach	Description	Duration
Step 1: Attribute coding	Highlight/note the basic information of the transcript, including setting, context, and participant demographics.	Simple, short
Step 2: Descriptive coding	Summarize the basic topic of a line or lines of data in the transcript. Choose from four approaches here: 2A: Structural coding—prior to data analysis, develop a set of codes based on the research question or review of the literature and assign these codes to a line(s) of data. 2B: In vivo—code a line(s) of the transcript using words or phrases found in the transcript. 2C: Process coding—note action found in transcripts using gerunds (-*ing* words). 2D: Values coding—infer the values and beliefs of the participants as described through the transcripts and make note of these as codes for a line(s) of the transcript.	Extensive, comprehensive
Step 3: Holistic coding	Assign either an entire piece of data or larger chunk of data with a macro-level code to describe it.	Macro-level review, short

to draft a summary of your research using the prompts below. You can either send this to your critical friend in advance of the meeting or use the prompts to guide your discussion.

Prompts for the action researcher (adapted from McNiff, 2016):

- What was my concern?

- What was my research question?

- Why was I concerned?

- What did I do about my concern?

- What are the outcomes?

- What are my provisional knowledge claims?

- What are my provisional conclusions about

    o the validity of my claims to knowledge?

    o the significance of what I am doing?

- What do I think could be improved?

- Where do I go from here?

Guidance for the Critical Friend:

As a critical friend, it is your job to provide open and honest feedback to the action researcher about his or her project. Be sure to listen carefully and probe for meaning. Provide feedback to the researcher based on the following categories (also adapted from McNiff, 2016):

- Comprehensibility—Do the research and the conclusions make sense? In what ways? How?

- Truthfulness—Does the research seem to be telling the truth? Are the claims or assertions based on evidence? What could be improved?

SHORTCUTS FOR QUALITATIVE DATA ANALYSIS IN ACTION RESEARCH OR MINI-STUDY

Practitioners pressed for time can benefit from adapting some practices from action research. Below are suggestions for conducting shortened forms of data analysis to inform your practice.

Analyze Your Research Journal

Set aside time to record in a researcher journal over the course of one week. You might choose to focus on implementing a new unit plan or teaching approach, or you may want to focus on a particular group of students or other aspect of classroom life. The point here is to collect as many details as possible throughout the week about the teaching and learning outcomes in your classroom. After the week is over, read back through your journal entries and make brief notes in the margins to highlight key characteristics or themes. Next, look across these notes to develop a few sentences to summarize the week. Jot these sentences down in the journal. Next, consider how you might proceed based on the journal entries you analyzed. How might you change your practice?

Analyze Preexisting Qualitative Data

Request a copy of your most recent teaching evaluations from an administrator or gather

Figure 6.2   Example of a Visual Diagram

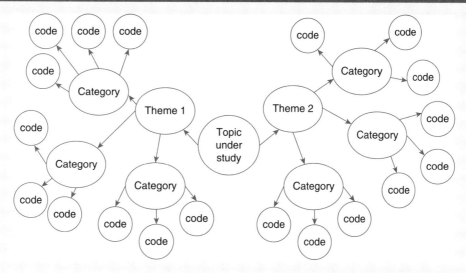

recent student evaluations. Make a photocopy that you can highlight and annotate by adding notes in the margins. Jot down key words or phrases that appear in the evaluations. Can you identify any key themes? Are there any notes in the evaluations that seem to repeat or can be easily categorized? For instance, can you note teaching practices, student behaviors, classroom climate, and so on?

Extension: Create a Visual Diagram

If you are able to gather multiple forms of data (e.g., research journal entries, teaching evaluations) and analyze them, create a visual diagram based on your analysis. First, begin by jotting down a list of the codes that you created. Next, combine codes into categories and then finally combine categories to create a list of themes or generalizations. Based on these lists, develop a visual diagram (see Figure 6.2). An example might be to create a web diagram.

APPENDICES

Appendix A: Focus Group Example Transcript (shortened)

Seventh-grade social studies

December 5, 2016

Context: Study about social studies teaching strategies

Interviewer: So do you remember what the compelling question was for this unit, for instance, on World War II? When you studied about Hitler?

Student 1: Oh . . . it was . . .

Student 2: How did World War II

Student 1: Something about, like, power . . .

Student 3: Change the world . . .

Student 2: Yeah, something about . . .

Student 1: I remember a supporting question was how did World War I lead into, create World War II.

Interviewer: Okay. So how did WWI lead into WWII. Do you remember the answer to that?

Student 3: The Treaty of Versailles . . .

Student 2: Yeah, they limited Germany and they were struggling and they saw Hitler as a solution. So they elected him and he had his ideas.

Student 1: We did this activity where you and a couple of friends are staying at a beach house; you guys make a giant mess. You have three options you can use to clean it up. First, you can have all your friends sit down, talk about it, and clean it up yourself. You can talk to the parents, and even though you'll get yelled at a lot you understand it's for the best. Or your friend has an older brother who's really good at fixing things and he could come help. So that way the parents aren't involved. So the idea is the first scenario with the doing it yourself that was . . .

Student 3: That was democracy.

Interviewer: Okay.

Student 1: That was democracy. The second one with the parents—the parents were the monarch.

Student 3: That's the Kaiser.

Student 1: And then the last one was Hitler.

Student 3: So, what was really funny was that we chose Hitler.

Interviewer: Why?

Student 1: Well, actually I chose the second one because I've had this conversation with a lot of my friends. If we're so immature that we're like . . . like we had this big discussion a few years ago. I don't think we need to go talk to the parents anymore. If we're mature enough to not go talk to the parents, then we're mature enough to not do whatever we're doing.

Interviewer: So that was one example of where they used a simulation, or a role play, or a scenario with you, right? So, is this different than the way you've learned social studies in the past, at all?

Student 1: Yeah, this is like how we've done it for the most part.

Student 2: Social studies has always been like worksheets . . .

Student 1: And videos.

Student 2: And videos . . .

Interviewer: Yeah. What do you do on the worksheets? What kind of questions or things do you do?

Student 1: We have primary source documents.

Student 2: Then there are documents that are like a poem or something or speech. And in the side notes, I guess, there are little questions that go with that paragraph.

Student 3: Then there are like five review questions at the end.

Interviewer: Okay, that helps me understand how you all approach these.

Appendix B: Focus Group Example Coded Transcript (shortened)

Seventh-grade social studies

December 5, 2016

Context: What are student experiences when social studies teachers integrate primary sources and inquiry questions into instruction? *[attribute coding: seventh grade, social studies, student experiences, and social studies teaching/pedagogy]*

Interviewer: So, do you remember what the compelling question was for this unit, for instance, on World War II? When you studied about Hitler?

Student 1: Oh . . . it was . . .

Student 2: How did World War II

Student 1: Something about, like, power . . .

Student 3: Change the world . . .

Student 2: Yeah, something about . . . *[structural coding: vague recollection]*

Student 1: I remember a supporting question was how did World War I lead into, create World War II.

Interviewer: Okay. So how did WWI lead into WWII. Do you remember the answer to that?

Student 3: The Treaty of Versailles . . . *[structural coding: content knowledge (CK)]*

Student 2: Yeah, they limited Germany and they were struggling and they saw Hitler as a solution. So they elected him and he had his ideas. *[structural coding: content knowledge (CK)]*

Student 1: We did this activity where you and a couple of friends are staying at a beach house; you guys make a giant mess. You have three options you can use to clean it up. First, you can have all your friends sit down, talk about it, and clean it up yourself. You can talk to the parents, and even though you'll get yelled at a lot you understand it's for the best. Or your friend

has an older brother who's really good at fixing things and he could come help. So that way the parents aren't involved. So the idea is the first scenario with the doing it yourself that was . . . *[process coding: personalizing; values coding: liked the scenario]*

Student 3: That was democracy. *[structural coding: content knowledge (CK)]*

Interviewer: Okay.

Student 1: That was democracy. The second one with the parents—the parents were the monarch. *[process coding: personalizing]*

Student 3: That's the Kaiser. *[structural coding: content knowledge (CK)]*

Student 1: And then the last one was Hitler.

Student 3: So what was really funny was that we chose Hitler. *[process coding: personalizing]*

Interviewer: Why?

Student 1: Well, actually I chose the second one because I've had this conversation with a lot of my friends. If we're so immature that we're like . . . like we had this big discussion a few years ago. I don't think we need to go talk to the parents anymore. If we're mature enough to not go talk to the parents, then we're mature enough to not do whatever we're doing. *[process coding: personalizing; values coding: liked scenario]*

Interviewer: So that was one example of where they used a simulation, or a role play, or a scenario with you, right? And so some of the other things that I've observed them use are photographs like this and texts, like primary source texts. To help answer questions. So, is this different than the way you've learned social studies in the past, at all?

Student 1: Yeah this is like how we've done it for the most part. *[process coding: continuing; structural coding: student experience]*

Student 2: Social studies has always been like worksheets . . . *[in vivo code: "worksheets"]*

Student 1: And videos. *[in vivo code: "videos"]*

Student 2: And videos . . .

Interviewer: Yeah. What do you do on the worksheets? Like what kind of questions or things do you do?

Student 1: We have primary source documents. *[in vivo code: "primary sources"; structural coding: primary sources]*

Student 2: Then their documents that are like a poem or something or speech. And in the side notes, I guess, there are little questions that go with that paragraph. *[in vivo code: "little questions"; process coding: answering questions]*

Student 3: Then there are like five review questions at the end. *[process coding: answering questions]*

Interviewer: Okay, that helps me understand how you all approach these.

CHAPTER 7

Quantitative Approaches to Data Collection and Analysis

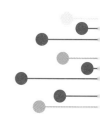

Guiding Questions

1. What are the affordances of using quantitative approaches to data collection and analysis for action researchers?
2. How can action researchers use standardized achievement data to inform their research studies?
3. How can teacher-created assessments inform action researchers?
4. To what extent can and should action researchers seek to pursue experimental research designs?
5. What are basic statistical analysis tools that action researchers can use?
6. What are key concerns in integrating surveys and questionnaires into action research studies?
7. How can quantitative content analysis inform the work of action researchers?
8. What options do action researchers have for integrating mixed methods designs into their work?

Keywords and Glossary

Criterion-referenced tests: measure student mastery of a predetermined set of standards or criteria. They are related to standards-referenced tests and standards-based assessment, which are intended to align with curriculum standards.

Formative assessment: ongoing and systematic assessment of student outcomes designed to provide teachers with real-time data. Formative assessments can be informal or formal and are used to design instruction to remediate gaps in student understanding.

Likert scales: also referred to as "Likert-type scales," these are ordinal scales designed to rank participant responses. These scales frequently appear in surveys and questionnaires.

Mean: is the average percentage of a series of numerical data points. The mean is derived by adding up a series of numerical data and dividing the sum by the number of data points.

Mode: refers to the most frequently occurring number or score in a list.

Norm-referenced tests: are "normed" to represent the average test scores of the cohort of test takers. Scores are representative of a student's relative rank among peers. These tests rank test takers along a bell curve.

Standard deviation: is the relative distance from the mean and is a measure used to understand the variability of data.

Value-added measures (VAMs): refer to changes in student test scores or achievement data and ascribe those changes to teacher performance.

Chapter Overview

In this era of data-based decision-making, teachers, schools, community groups, and policy makers often rely on quantitative statistics to describe and make sense of outcomes of practice. This is especially true when measuring student performance. For instance, quantitative measures are increasingly used to measure teacher "effectiveness" and school funding may be associated with student achievement outcomes. Schools in some states are given letter grades (A–F) based on their ability to "make growth" on value-added measures. This approach to measuring school performance is popular, although we know a more comprehensive, broad-based approach to assessment that includes ongoing formative and summative assessments can be even more accurate at measuring student-learning outcomes.

In many ways action research is an antidote to the narrow approach to assessing students, teachers, and schools that has gripped current educational reform initiatives, including high-stakes testing. Action research provides teachers and other stakeholders with opportunities to reflect, study, and understand what the numbers mean. According to Merrow (2001),

> The idea that student performance on standardized, norm-referenced, machine-scored tests is the primary indicator of school quality, and the principal measure of accountability, has been with us for about 40 years. It shows few signs of going away. We've grown accustomed to international, national, state, and local comparisons based on test scores, and we rarely look into the *why* of a number. (n.p.)

Action research provides a systematic and intentional approach to exploring the why of assessment results for individuals and groups of students, teachers, and schools.

Quantitative data can both provide a starting point for an action research study and serve as invaluable data to action researchers as they peel apart the complex layers of practice. For example, in order to make sense of practice and its impact, researchers may choose to analyze preexisting quantitative data such as assessment data from high-stakes tests or to gather additional quantitative data through surveys and questionnaires. Action researchers should "treat statistics as one of an array of many tools that can help teacher researchers gain insight into their data and communicate them effectively to others" (Mills, 2011, p. 139). Quantitative data expressed as numerical statistics may efficiently and succinctly provide an outline of patterns and outcomes.

Working With Assessment Data

A readily available source of quantitative data in schools is assessment data, including from high-stakes standardized tests as well as from teacher-created assessments. Setting aside political issues related to high-stakes, standardized tests, action researchers may be able to mine this data to look for patterns regarding student achievement. Further inquiry, for instance, through qualitative interviews, observation, and document analysis, might provide insight into the root issues underlying student test scores. Teacher-created assessment data similarly provide rich opportunities for narrowing the focus of an action research project to specific teaching strategies and student outcomes. An analysis of teacher-created assessments might even prompt a study about the usefulness and accuracy of these assessments in determining student-learning outcomes. Action researchers can make good use of both external assessment data (e.g., state and district assessment) and internal, teacher-created assessment data or other forms of quantitative data in their action research projects.

Standardized Tests

Standardized tests provide student achievement data. There are two types of these tests: norm-referenced tests and criterion-referenced tests. Many of the most frequently recognizable national assessment tests are **norm-referenced tests**, meaning the data are reported as percentile ranks and are intended to demonstrate the relative performance of students. Examples of norm-referenced tests include IQ tests, the Stanford Achievement Test, the California Achievement Test (CAT), and the Iowa Test of Basic Skills. It is important to note that norm-referenced tests rank test takers on a bell curve. In some cases, a test report from a criterion-referenced test may provide information about both the number of items a student answered correctly as well as their percentile rank compared to other test takers. It is important to note that test questions often only survey a portion of content from a subject. Even more complicated, often just a sample of questions are used to "norm" test taker scores. In other words, "one more question right or wrong can cause a big change in the student's score" (Fairtest.org, n.d.). Today some test providers, including the Iowa Test of Basic Skills, also provide "student growth" scores. Yet growth scores are only helpful if the same population of students is assessed from year to year. By its nature, a norm-referenced test refers to the cohort of test takers in a given year. It is therefore difficult to compare scores of this year's third graders, for instance, to last year's third graders.

Criterion-Referenced Tests

Criterion-referenced tests measure student mastery of a predetermined set of standards or criteria. The tests are used to determine whether a student has learned content associated with a specific course or grade level. Here, "cut-off" scores are determined by a group of experts and are subjective in nature (see Fairtest.org, n.d.). These tests are most often referred to as end-of-grade or end-of-course tests and may be unique to individual states. They are related to standards-referenced tests and standards-based assessment, which are intended to align with curriculum standards.

It is important for teachers and other stakeholders to take into account the limitations of both norm-referenced and criterion-referenced standardized tests. For the most part, they rely mainly on multiple-choice test items with some short-answer questions. Standardized tests may not accurately assess all of the knowledge and skills that we hope students will learn through their education, either due to their format or because they are culturally biased (see, for example, Au, 2016; Darling-Hammond, 2007). And, even though norm-referenced tests rank students on a curve, they are sometimes incorrectly used to assess whether students meet certain curricular standards.

Value-Added Measures

Regardless of the type of assessment, the data generated often provide a snapshot of an entire school and the achievement of its students. Previously this was referred to as Annual Yearly Progress (AYP) during the No Child Left Behind (NCLB) era. Today, with the passage of the federal Every Student Succeeds Act (ESSA), states are no longer required to produce AYP but are required to develop some form of an accountability system. As a result, many states have adopted value-added measures (VAMs) intended to measure the impact of the teacher on student-learning outcome or "growth" (see also Gaurino, Reckase, & Wooldridge, 2015; Harris, 2011). Teachers in states with VAMs will receive reports about individual student data as well as estimations of their impact on student-learning outcomes.

Standardized Tests and Opportunities for Action Researchers

Action researchers can use standardized test score data in a variety of ways. First, achievement data can provide the impetus for a study. For example, the data can provide an overview of achievement patterns within a school and classroom. Since these data are publicly available to community members and policy makers, it is important for action researchers to help make sense of what the scores reveal. For example, when educators drill down into test results to examine the achievement of various subgroups (e.g., ethnic, gender, special services), particular patterns may appear. If criterion-referenced tests are used, the data can also highlight areas of need regarding content instruction. For example, educators may note that students have an uneven understanding of course concepts based on patterns in student responses. Most end-of-grade or end-of-course test reports provide a breakdown of scores based on categories of content or curriculum objectives.

Analyzing Achievement Test Data

After a preliminary examination of achievement test data, action researchers may embark on a study to determine why certain achievement patterns exist and whether these patterns in test scores align with the realities of classroom instruction. Based on their analysis, they can develop strategies to confront these inequities. According to Henning, Stone, and Kelly (2009), standardized achievement data can be used to compare individuals or groups of individuals to the norm. Here "norm" refers to the relative achievement of students compared to their peers. By analyzing achievement test scores as reported in test score reports, teachers can identify areas of strength and weakness for individual students. Through this analysis, teachers can determine areas for remediation or enrichment. Similarly, teachers can compare groups of students to the norm. Here, "the purpose of this analysis would be to adjust lesson or unit plans at the classroom level or to adjust instructional programs at the grade, building or district levels" (Henning et al., 2009, p. 115). By comparing achievement tests scores for groups of students to the norm, teachers and administrators can identify potential gaps in the curriculum and areas for further development. This may also lead to discussions about the extent to which the achievement test data align with data from classroom instruction and classroom-based assessments.

Comparing Subgroups and Longitudinal Trends

Action researchers may also decide to disaggregate achievement test score data based on other factors, including gender, ethnic identity, socioeconomic status (as reflected in free and reduced-price lunch status) and other relevant characteristics (such as an identified learning disability, etc.). By comparing subgroups of students to the norm, teachers and administrators might begin to better understand the experiences of specific groups of students and use action research to find remedies for uneven achievement patterns (Henning et al., 2009). New teaching strategies, professional development initiatives, and support services for students might be developed based on this analysis. The data can also be used to determine strategies for creating a more comprehensive approach to assessment that goes beyond standardized tests.

Action researchers can also use standardized assessment tests at the end of an action research study to measure student-learning outcomes and to develop a longitudinal understanding of student learning over time. Through correlating achievement test data, action researchers can determine whether relationships exist between standardized test scores and other measures of student achievement. For example, Henning et al. (2009) recommend comparing standardized achievement test scores to "other school measures, such as grades, attendance, discipline interventions, or other standardized achievement test scores" (p. 124). For example, by comparing standardized test score data to grades (or GPA), action researchers can determine whether high-achieving students are also doing well in the classroom. Similarly, they can make comparisons across other data points to look for patterns and identify areas in need of further study. Based on their analysis they can also begin to make informed judgments about the usefulness of the standardized tests for site-based decision-making.

Finally, most standardized test providers release exam items for teachers to reference. These released items can be adapted for use by action researchers to evaluate student learning in the classroom. By using validated test questions, action researchers can develop measurement tools to use in their own research. For example, a teacher could design an in-class assessment of student learning using released items from the National Assessment of Educational Progress (NAEP) assessments or the New York Regents exams (both readily available online).

Teacher-Created Assessments

Of course, teachers and action researchers do not wait for end-of-course or standardized assessments to begin assessing student-learning outcomes. Rather, quality instruction includes ongoing, systematic formative and summative assessments to monitor student progress. **Formative assessments** may be informal (e.g., question-and-answer sessions or whole-group instruction in class) or formal (periodic and ongoing assignments such as homework to check for student understanding). Summative assessment most often occurs at the end of a unit of study, for instance, as a unit test, weekly spelling test, or final exam test. Formative and summative assessments can take many forms: They can be multiple choice, short answer, written reports, or project based.

Teacher-created assessments provide a rich source of data for action researchers. This data can be analyzed in the aggregate—for instance, monitoring the progress of a whole group or class over time. It can also be analyzed for individual students or a sample of students based on a particular criterion established by the research question. Rather than view assessments or tests as punitive tools designed to "weed" students out or as behavior modification tools, here assessment data serve as a diagnostic tool to monitor student learning and teaching effectiveness. Student assessment data can provide as much information about teacher behaviors and pedagogy as they can about student outcomes.

Action researchers may be interested in analyzing the efficacy of teacher-created assessments (e.g., whether the test or assignment provides a fair and accurate measure of student learning outcomes). In order to analyze teacher-created assessments, action researchers use test blueprints to map the content and skills assessed in the test items or assigned activities. (Note: This is different from the common approach to using a test blueprint to design an assessment. Rather, here it is used to identify patterns in the questions or activities contained in an assessment.) Often by completing a test blueprint, action researchers find interesting information about the efficacy of the assessment itself, such as whether the test evenly assesses student learning across content or whether some areas are emphasized or overemphasized. For example, if a multiple-choice test includes several questions about one learning objective, it can create a situation akin to double jeopardy for students—if they do not understand a concept, but the assessment has more than one item focused on the concept, they will be unfairly penalized.

Developing Pre- and Posttests

Beyond analyzing the efficacy of teacher-created assessments, action researchers may choose to use assessments to gather data about student-learning outcomes. It may be useful, for instance, for action researchers to create pre- and posttests to monitor student outcomes. Pretests are used to develop a baseline understanding of student prior knowledge and motivation to learn. Posttests, in turn, are used to monitor student learning outcomes and mastery of concepts at various points throughout the action research project. If the intention is to assess student learning outcomes (factual content, concepts, and skills), then there should be items that are similar or identical appearing on the pre- and posttests. Similarity across questions will make it easier to make direct comparisons between student responses. While action researchers can integrate pre- and posttests into their studies, they should think carefully about the extent to which they want to pursue experimental or quasi-experimental methods, including the use of control groups in their studies.

Suggestions for Rethinking Control Groups and Interventions

Pursuing experimental methods in action research may be undesirable as well as difficult to achieve. According to Mills (2011),

> Action researchers must not confuse the quantitative collection of data with the application of a quantitative research design. Experimental quantitative research requires students to be randomly assigned to a control group or an experimental group, and involves manipulation of the independent variables in order to control group assignments. (p. 89)

Not only is it difficult to achieve random variability in the regular classroom, it also seems to be unethical for action researchers. While it may be tempting to compare across students or classes to determine whether an intervention is working, it is not wise to withhold an experimental teaching activity from a group of students that you think may benefit those students. Rather, teachers must always provide all of their students with the best quality teaching and learning activities available to them. At the same time, it is too difficult to adequately "control" for differences between students. Students are unique individuals with their own backgrounds, contexts, and experiences. Action researchers must meet students where they are rather than attempt to control for differences across students (see also Elliott, 2007).

For action researchers interested in isolating the impact of a specific pedagogical technique or instructional resource, first consider collecting baseline data before implementing a change in practice. By comparing the before and after, action researchers may be able to attribute changing outcomes in the classroom to the research design. For example, a teacher might identify set blocks of time (e.g., a unit of study) to engage in bringing about change and studying that change. We refer to this as *experiential change* in Figure 7.1 to connote the outcomes of trial and error, investigation, and examination of changes in practice.

In this example of an action research design, a comparative approach is used to contrast the status quo with experiences related to changing elements of practice. This approach will provide rich data to help action researchers understand cause and effect in their studies. Here a variety of assessment data as well as other qualitative techniques can be used to gather evidence of participant experiences. Within this design, quantitative data from teacher evaluation instruments may also be used.

Teacher Evaluation Instruments

In addition to student achievement data, administrators often evaluate teacher performance using protocols or evaluation standards set at the school, district, or state level. At the national level, teachers may choose to participate in the National Board Certification process based on a set of standards developed by the Interstate Teacher Assessment and Support Consortium (InTASC). Locally, action researchers can use quantitative data from teacher evaluations to examine patterns across a school or longitudinally for individuals or groups of teachers. Again, these data can be used to identify areas of concern and to launch an action research project. They can also be used over the course of an action research project to monitor teacher outcomes. Of course, teacher evaluation data are highly personal and often subject to privacy and personnel laws. For action researchers interested in analyzing previously collected evaluation instruments, they must strip away any identifiers from the data and refer to aggregate patterns in the data. Action researchers must also seek appropriate permissions from institutional review boards (IRBs).

An alternative suggestion would be for action researchers to create an observation protocol based on standardized and validated teacher evaluation instruments to collect additional data related to the topic of an action research project. Options include using the Danielson Framework, the Reformed Teaching Observation Protocol (RTOP), or the Teaching Dimensions Observation Protocol (see Suggested Web-Based Resources at the end of this chapter for more information about these

Figure 7.1 Example Research Design		
Unit A – baseline data collection >	Unit B – experiential change round 1 with data collection >	Unit C – experiential change round 2 with data collection
Unit A – status quo instruction with data collection >	Unit B – integrating inquiry-based instruction using web-based resources round 1 with data collection >	Unit C – integrating inquiry-based instruction using web-based resources round 2 and data collection

observation protocols). Action researchers can adapt these protocols to meet the parameters of their action research study and to systematically collect classroom observation data. (See, for example, the research design featured in Figure 7.1.)

Surveys and Questionnaires

In addition to teacher evaluation instruments, surveys and questionnaires provide rich sources of quantitative data for action researchers. By deploying a survey, action researchers can gather feedback from a large number of participants relatively quickly. Surveys and questionnaires can be used at the beginning of a project to help refine research ideas and to collect general information about participants and the research context. These data collection tools can be used to collect baseline data and to help define the direction of a research study or to initiate a change in practice. At the same time, Stringer (2014) recommends that surveys be used in the later stages of action research "for extending the data collection process to a broader range of participants" and "to check whether information acquired from participants in the first cycles of a process is relevant to other individuals and groups" (p. 118). The data yielded by surveys and questionnaires is often easy to represent in frequency counts and can provide information for future study. Regardless of when researchers integrate surveys and questionnaires into the data collection process, they must be designed thoughtfully and with the research questions in mind if they are to provide rich data for action research.

Developing Survey Instruments

Similar to the process of designing a test or an assessment as a diagnostic tool for student learning, action researchers should first develop a blueprint before designing a survey instrument. This blueprint should reflect the focus of the action research question(s) and include a list of "the issues to be included," "information to be obtained," and "the respondents to be included in the survey sample"

(Stringer, 2014, p. 118). From this starting point, researchers should create at least one question for each of the issues listed. Once questions are developed, it is important to review the wording of questions. Some good rules of thumb for developing and implementing surveys include the following:

- Keep the questions short and to the point.
  - State questions in clear and unambiguous terms.
  - State questions in positive rather than negative terms.
  - Do not include jargon or technical terms that may be unfamiliar to respondents.
- Test the instrument with a small pilot group of respondents.
- Revise and edit as needed.
- Launch the survey.

Survey Formats and Question Types

There are several formats and question choices to use when creating survey instruments. One common format is to provide a matrix or rating scale for participants. Researchers can then weigh participant responses using a scale, such as a **Likert scale** (see Figure 7.2).

Other options for survey questions include using fixed-response questions in which the survey developer provides a limited list of choices or dual-response questions such as those requiring "yes" or "no" answers. Another option is to include open-ended questions. These questions "allow the respondents to provide a seemingly limitless number of responses" (Mertler, 2014, p. 134). They may provide more accurate information about participant experiences since respondents are not constrained by predetermined responses. At the same time, open-ended survey questions will yield data that need to be analyzed using qualitative content analysis or inductive coding techniques. Table 7.1 provides a list of example survey questions, all focused on the same research topic—understanding student

Figure 7.2   Sample Question Stems for Likert Scale Survey Questions

To what extent do you agree with the following statement? (5 being strongly agree, 1 being strongly disagree)

5 strongly agree	4 agree	3 neutral (neither agree or disagree)	2 disagree	1 strongly disagree

Table 7.1   Example Survey Question Types

Likert Scale

Rate your level of agreement with the following statements:

1.	I feel confident in my ability to analyze primary sources.	5	4	3	2	1
2.	I am able to learn about history through the analysis of primary sources.	5	4	3	2	1
3.	I enjoy analyzing primary sources in history class.	5	4	3	2	1

Fixed Response

1. Do you feel confident in your ability to analyze primary sources?

   Yes No

2. Do you feel you learn history content when you analyze primary sources?

   Yes No

3. Do you enjoy analyzing primary sources in history class?

   Yes No

Open Ended

1. Do you feel confident in your ability to analyze primary sources? Why or why not?

2. How does analyzing primary sources affect your ability to learn history?

3. Do you enjoy analyzing primary sources? Why or why not?

efficacy using primary sources in the social studies classroom. This table provides a sense of the direction and scope as well as affordances and limitations of each type of question.

Web-Based Survey Tools

There are many web-based survey tools available for action researchers to use. These include proprietary software tools such as Qualtrics, SurveyMonkey, and Zoho Survey (see Suggested Web-Based Resources at the end of this chapter). Most of these tools offer some version of a free account, but it might be limited—for instance, only allowing the user to create a 10-question survey. The Google suite also offers Google Forms, which can be used to create surveys. While this tool is relatively easy to use and the results are displayed in a spreadsheet, the data are not automatically analyzed as in other tools. Once again, action researchers must weigh the affordances and limitations of various tools available and determine the best match for their project.

Considering Advantages and Limitations of Surveys

Of course, there are advantages and disadvantages to using surveys and questionnaires. Advantages include being able to collect a range of data relatively quickly. This can be especially helpful to researchers in the exploratory stages of a research study. Action researchers can use data from surveys to refine their research questions and to begin to identify patterns. At the same time, surveys are relatively easy for participants to use and the format is generally recognizable. They also enable researchers to collect anonymous data from participants, which may yield information not readily attainable through face-to-face and one-on-one interviews.

While there are many advantages to using surveys in qualitative research, there are also drawbacks. First, participants may not respond honestly to survey questions. This phenomenon, referred to as "social desirability bias," suggests that survey respondents often overestimate positive behaviors and underreport negative behaviors (Karp & Brockington, 2005; Persson & Solevid, 2014). Second, the manner in which questions are posed could influence participant responses, especially if the researcher poses subjective or biased questions. At the same time, researchers must be careful about providing questions that match the reading level of the audience, ensuring anonymity and providing participants with enough time to complete the surveys. Action researchers must avoid posing too many questions so their respondents do not get fatigued. They must also aim for high response rates in order to accurately reflect the experiences of the targeted population. A 75% response rate is desirable.

As researchers collect data from surveys, they can further weigh the affordances and limitations of the data collection tools they are using when they begin to engage in statistical analysis of the results. By determining the measures of central tendency in the data they collect, action researchers can begin to identify patterns and gaps. Based on their findings, they can seek additional data to provide a rich understanding of the phenomena under study.

Statistical Analysis
....

Once quantitative data are collected, action researchers must collate the data and compute appropriate statistical measures. Basic quantitative data analysis includes identifying the **mean** (or average), **mode**, **standard deviation**, and, perhaps, the maximum and minimum values of a series of numerical data. The mean, mode, and standard deviation are measures of central tendency. These measures allow researchers to distill an entire set of numbers into a representative figure or finding. For example, according to Mills (2011), "it [a statistical measure] allows us to talk in generalities and to compare how the students in our class have performed 'on average' in comparison to other students or over a given time period" (p. 140).

Measures of Central Tendency

Procedures for calculating a mean or an average are usually familiar to educators, especially since teachers average grades in their grade books. However, mode and standard deviation may be less familiar. The mode refers to the most frequently occurring number or score in a list. In some instances, it may be useful for researchers to identify the most frequently occurring response of participants, such as on a test item or survey question.

Standard deviation, put simply, is the relative distance from the mean and is a measure used to understand the variability of data. A smaller standard deviation suggests that most of the scores skewed in similar directions. This is helpful when taken into consideration with the mean. For example, "for the classroom teacher seeking to confirm mastery of subject matter on a criterion-referenced test (teacher made test), a higher mean and smaller standard deviation would be a desirable outcome" (Mills, 2011, p. 141). Calculating the mean, mode, and standard deviation of quantitative data provide action researchers with multiple approaches to analyzing data to look for patterns and derive meaning.

Action researchers can compute measures of central tendency or the basic quantitative analysis procedures described above using Excel spreadsheets. Recent versions of Excel include easy-to-access reference lists of formulas, which researchers insert into spreadsheets or databases. Some of the web-based survey tools mentioned above, such as SurveyMonkey and Qualtrics, will automatically analyze basic statistics for survey responses and develop graphs.

Statistical Software

Most of the statistical analysis action researchers will need to conduct can be done using Excel spreadsheets. However, action researchers may have access to more robust, computer-based statistical software such as STATA or SPSS. It may be desirable to use these programs if action researchers are working with large data sets. Most software programs offer online tutorials, including YouTube videos to guide users through the process of conducting quantitative analysis using their software. Action researchers also use quantitative analysis software to create charts, diagrams, and tables to present quantitative findings in visual forms. Visualizations of data assist researchers in drawing conclusions about research findings and in communicating findings to readers (Koshy, 2010). These visualization strategies can extend beyond numerical data to include text-based data, as in quantitative content analysis.

Quantitative Content Analysis

In addition to analyzing numerical data from assessments and surveys, action researchers use quantitative content analysis to track occurrences and make comparisons across data. Content analysis can be applied to text-based data, including observation field notes, interview transcripts, and samples of student work. Using content analysis, an action researcher can record on a spreadsheet the number of times an event occurred, the number of people involved, and the range of activities recorded. For example, if an action researcher analyzed the content of field notes from a class observation, she might tally the number of times students asked questions, moved about the room, appeared to be "on task," and so on. To provide more nuanced analysis, she may also tally the types of questions students asked or answered (e.g., memorization, evaluation, or reflection questions) and the type of tasks students completed. Once the researcher tallies observation data, she can use the numerical data to identify patterns or themes (e.g., the teachers and students mainly asked and answered questions that required memorization).

Content analysis is useful for making comparisons as well. Returning to the example above, a simple tally of the types of questions asked and answered could reveal trends related to gender, ethnicity, and ability grouping. Does the teacher call on boys and girls at the same rate? Are the questions that are asked qualitatively similar or different? Do all students have an opportunity to respond to questions, regardless of ability? Researchers could conduct this same type of analysis on field notes or other qualitative data from multiple observations to identify trends over time.

Content analysis provides a relatively straightforward approach to analyzing a large set of qualitative data in a relatively quick amount of time. It is important to note that it may be most useful for action researchers to balance quantitative content analysis with qualitative analysis of key themes to determine why patterns are occurring in the data.

Mixed Methods Approaches

Since action research is an intentional and systematic approach to studying issues related to practice, action researchers are likely to collect and analyze both quantitative and qualitative data over the course of their projects. Unless the quantitative research design is quasi-experimental (which is often difficult to achieve in the midst of the messy world of everyday practice as we discussed above), most action research projects will use quantitative data to either inform qualitative data or the reverse. According to Creswell and Plano (2007), there are four main types of mixed methods designs: "the Triangulation Design, the Embedded Design, the Explanatory Design, and the Exploratory Design" (p. 59). Table 7.2 briefly describes these four types of mixed methods design.

Across these four types of mixed methods designs, the aim is to create a thick description of the area of practice that is under study by collecting a range of data

Vignette: Rocket Math

Using Mixed Methods to Understand Assessment

A local K–8 school recently undertook a study to explore math programs that would improve math automaticity for students. After reviewing Iowa Assessment test scores, the administrators and teachers noted areas of concern in math computation. They attributed these scores to a lack of automaticity or fluency in math facts. Teachers in the upper grades felt students were slow to complete complex math problems such as algebraic equations because they had not mastered basic math facts. As a result, the teachers and administrators explored a variety of options for math programs to supplement their regular instruction. After much exploration, they integrated a timed math program across the grade levels. This comprehensive program centered on a series of leveled worksheets with timed math problems (addition, subtraction, or multiplication). When students successfully met their goal on a level, they moved up to the next level.

After one semester of integrating Rocket Math, a small group of teachers in the early grades (K–2) conducted an action research study about their integration of the new math program. Their research revealed both affordances and limitations of for their students. They found that for a percentage of their students, math computation improved and students seemed to be motivated by the program. These students seemed to like the challenge of moving up from level to level. On the other hand, they found that for a percentage of their students the program created anxiety. Students who were not able to move up a level after several tries seemed frustrated and often gave up. They also found that some students tried to cheat during the timed tests. Finally, they were concerned that not all of their students were learning the appropriate math facts for the grade level. After 2 years of integrating the math program, the administrators felt that the program had helped the school improve its Iowa test scores in math. Yet the action research demonstrated a mixed picture. The school needed to put modifications in place so that all students could succeed in the math curriculum.

Table 7.2 Four Types of Mixed Methods Design	
Triangulation	Quantitative and qualitative data are collected simultaneously
Embedded	Either qualitative data are embedded in a quantitative design or quantitative data are embedded in a qualitative design
Explanatory	Quantitative data are collected first, followed by qualitative data
Exploratory	Qualitative data are collected first, followed by quantitative data

Source: Adapted from Creswell & Plano 2007.

and providing multiple types of data analysis. The choice in methodology and the scope of the project are determined by the research question posed by the action researcher. Since action research is a cycle, researchers may choose to refine their approach through each new cycle.

Chapter Reflection

As the vignette suggests, quantitative data analysis can be extremely useful to action researchers. It can spark a study by providing numerical data related to a problem of practice. Not only has this type of data become central to contemporary education reforms, but it is also used increasingly to make judgments about teacher and student performance. There is perhaps no shortage of quantitative data being produced and used by educational stakeholders to make "data-based" decisions. Action researchers have an opportunity to lead larger conversations about the usefulness of these data as well as about current educational reform movements that rely on quantitative measures by helping us understand the "why" behind the numbers.

CHAPTER SUMMARY

- Action research provides teachers and other stakeholders with opportunities to study and understand the meaning behind the quantitative data generated by contemporary educational reform initiatives, including standardized testing, value-added measures, and other evaluations of teacher and student performance.

- Action researchers can utilize a variety of quantitative data in their projects, including standardized achievement data, teacher-created assessments, surveys and questionnaires, and quantitative content analysis, to initiate a study, form the basis of a study, and determine the outcomes of a study.

- Action researchers must use caution when considering experimental approaches to their research design.

- Measures of central tendency, including mean (or average), mode, and standard deviation, enable researchers to distill large sets of data into representative figures.

- There are several mixed methods approaches action researchers use to blend quantitative and qualitative data collection and analysis techniques.

SUGGESTED WEB-BASED RESOURCES ————

Information About Standardized Testing

Testing, Assessment, and Excellence

http://www.pbs.org/wgbh/pages/frontline/shows/schools/testing/merrow.html

National Center for Fair & Open Testing

http://www.fairtest.org/

Criterion- and Standards-Referenced Tests

http://www.fairtest.org/facts/csrtests.html

Norm-Referenced Achievement Tests

http://fairtest.org/facts/nratests.htm

Observation Protocols

Danielson Framework

http://www.danielsongroup.org/framework/

Reformed Teaching Observation Protocol

http://physicsed.buffalostate.edu/AZTEC/RTOP/RTOP_full/using_RTOP_1.html

Teaching Dimensions Observation Protocol

http://tdop.wceruw.org/

Survey Tools

SurveyMonkey

https://www.surveymonkey.com/

Zoho Survey

https://www.zoho.com/survey/

Qualtrics

https://www.qualtrics.com/

Google Forms

https://gsuite.google.com/products/forms

QUESTIONS AND ACTIVITIES ————

Reflection Questions

1. What are the affordances and limitations of using quantitative data collection and analysis techniques in action research?

2. How might mixed methods designs balance out these affordances and limitations?

3. Why is it important for educational stakeholders to seek to understand the *why* behind quantitative data produced by educational reform initiatives such as standardized testing, value-added measures, and other measures of student and teacher performance?

Practice Activities

Activity 7A: Creating a Test Blueprint

A good assessment, including a teacher-created test, is developed carefully in order to avoid redundancy and bias. In this activity, you will use a test blueprint to analyze and assess a teacher-created test.

1. Ask a teacher colleague to provide you with a sample test (multiple choice is preferred) along with a list of the curriculum objectives or standards.

2. On a separate page or on an Excel spreadsheet, create a table. This will be your test blueprint.

   a. Across the top of the table, list question types using Bloom's taxonomy: knowledge (memory), understand (describe), apply, analyze, evaluate, and create.

   b. Down the side of the table, list the curriculum objectives or standards.

3. Once you have completed your test blueprint, return to the teacher-created test. Analyze each question and place the corresponding number for each test item on the blueprint.

4. Once you have analyzed all of the test items, answer the following reflection questions:

   a. What patterns do you notice in the test items?

   b. Are there any areas of the curriculum that are over- or undertested?

   c. What recommendations do you have for the teacher to improve the test?

5. To add an additional layer of complexity, code the test questions to highlight the key topic or concept being assessed. Next, return to your blueprint. Can you identify patterns in question type related to content? What are the implications for practice?

6. If it is an option, share your findings with the teacher who gave you the test. Discuss.

Activity 7B: Creating a Survey

After reviewing the steps for creating a survey in this chapter, design your own survey instrument in this activity.

1. Review your research question and aims.

2. Determine the participants you will target to complete your survey.

3. Create a strategy for recruiting participants, including collecting contact information and developing a script to recruit participants.

4. Choose a format for your survey and a delivery tool (e.g., paper based or web based).

5. Create a survey blueprint in which you list the major issues/topics about which you hope to survey participants.

6. Use the survey blueprint to draft 10–15 survey items. Experiment with various types of items including Likert-type scales, open-ended questions, and closed questions.

7. Once you have developed your survey questions, review the "rules of thumb" for creating survey items in this chapter. Edit your survey questions as needed.

8. Pilot your survey with a small sample of participants. If possible, conduct brief follow-up interviews with participants to determine whether survey items were clear.

9. Revise your survey as needed.

Activity 7C: Creating a Pre- and Post-Research Design

In this activity, you will refer back to Figure 7.1, Example Research Design. The aim here is to map out a research design that makes use of baseline and experiential changes in practice.

1. Refer back to your research questions and research purposes.

2. Complete the following table:

Description	Baseline	Round 1	Round 2
Experiential change (the change in practice to be implemented)	N/A		
Data to be collected (quantitative and qualitative)			
Data analysis techniques			
Describe how this stage informs the next	N/A		

Sharing Findings

Reflection and the Action Research Report

Guiding Questions

1. What have you learned from your experiences as an action researcher?
2. Why is it important for action researchers to share their findings?
3. What are steps that action researchers can take to make the process of writing a final report more manageable?
4. What options are available for action researchers to share their findings?
5. What strategies can action researchers use to improve the trustworthiness of their findings?
6. How can you build on your experiences to become an advocate for you and for others?
7. What additional lines of inquiry should you pursue?

Keywords and Glossary

Collective impact: is the process of linking with allies to leverage individual expertise and resources to make a greater impact and solve a social problem.

Critical friends: provide formative feedback throughout the research process and can be invaluable in identifying issues of bias and subjectivity.

Member checking: involves the process of going back to participants to have them review transcripts or final reports to ensure that the evidence and documentation accurately capture their experiences.

Peer review: can include both peer editing or a more formal, double blind review of a project often for an academic journal or conference presentation.

Reflection: as it relates to action research, refers to "reflection in action" and "reflection on action." Here, reflection is systematic, intentional, and designed to improve practice.

Saturation: refers to the process of collecting data over the course of a study until you reach the point at which you have thoroughly "saturated" the results.

Theory of action: summarizes findings from action research to describe practice.

Trustworthiness: is the logic that undergirds and guides an action research study, fundamentally influencing the validity of the findings. There are many strategies action researchers can use to improve the trustworthiness of their findings, including triangulation, saturation, member checks, critical friends, and peer review.

Reflection on Findings

Reflection is one of the most important prerequisites of professional growth, yet rarely as educators do we have the opportunity to slow down and reflect on our work and its impact. Because of the nature of action research, reflection is naturally built into the process.

For simplicity, we have referred to the action research cycle as a fairly straightforward set of steps beginning and ending with problem posing, as on the left side of in Figure 8.1. However, the second, overlapping cycle provides a more holistic sense of the manner in which these steps interconnect. Throughout an action research project, reflection is infused across the action and observation phases

Figure 8.1   Two Views of the Action Research Cycle

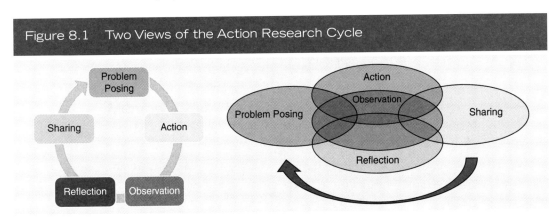

and plays an important part in problem posing and sharing findings. This chapter focuses on the process by which action researchers reflect on their findings and develop a formal, written report about those findings.

Reflection as it relates to action research has been variously referred to as "reflection in action" and "reflection on action" (Schön, 1983). Both of these phrases emphasize the notion that reflection occurs in the act of practice, as well as about practice. Action researchers, through collecting data and reflecting on that data, systematically and intentionally examine their actions and the consequences of those actions. Here, reflection takes on more import than the everyday reflection we engage in as we drive home from work or head into the classroom. Rather, within action research, reflection is directed, intentional, and designed to move practice forward. To promote the practice of more intentional reflection, action researchers develop habits such as keeping action research journals or regularly engaging in conversation with **critical friends**.

For many action researchers, new problems to explore will become obvious over the course of study. It is often the case during action research that the more you learn, the more questions you will have. In order to engage in additional study, it will be important to proceed systematically through the process of posing new questions and planning for future study. Again, it will be helpful to seek insight from relevant research literature, key stakeholders, and other informants or potential collaborators. It is important to leverage your previous action research to move forward and continue to work for positive change.

It may be helpful to use a protocol to guide systematic reflection on your findings as well as next steps. Use this series of prompts to guide both written reflection and oral dialogue about practice:

1. What did I intend to do?

2. What seemed to be the outcomes of my actions?

3. How do I know this occurred?

4. What additional or new questions do I have?

5. What are my next steps?

These questions draw attention to what has been done and what is next. This simple exercise can move practitioners toward more intentional action and more thoughtful reflection about that action.

In the previous chapters, we were very specific about the process of collecting data. Data or evidence forms the basis on which action researchers can begin to answer research questions and to assess the consequences of their actions. After data collection and analysis, action researchers write about the findings of their projects to share with a larger audience.

Writing as a Form of Reflection

In many ways, writing about a project provides yet another opportunity for analysis. Writing allows researchers to tap into cognitive processes that deepen conceptual understanding. According to Mills (2011),

> The value in writing up your research is that the process of writing requires the writer to clarify meaning—to choose words carefully, thoughtfully describe that which is experienced or seen, reflect on experiences, and refine phrasing when putting words on a page. (p. 171)

The writing process, including deliberating over language to best express meaning, may provide new insights about the data collected.

Reflection through writing also provides action researchers with a voice. By sharing findings widely, with a broader audience, action researchers claim their professional expertise. According to Stringer (2014), action research "seeks to give voice to people who have previously been silent research subjects" (p. 213). Action research fundamentally shifts the relationship between practitioners and research institutions by engaging practitioners in the generation of research and new knowledge. The shift from research subject to researcher is fundamental. It provides practitioners with agency to guide the research rather than be a participant or study subject.

Addressing the Theory–Practice Divide

The process of conducting action research and sharing the findings has the potential to close the theory–practice divide. According to Mertler (2014), "sharing the results—either formally or informally—is the real activity that helps to bridge the divide between research and application" (p. 245). Whereas traditional research reports are written from the perspective of outside researchers, action research focuses on insider knowledge. This knowledge is essential for understanding practical applications of educational theory. Closing the gap between theory and practice depends on understanding everyday experiences to make informed judgments about practice. As a result, "the outcomes of the [action] research make the experience and perspectives of ordinary people directly available to stakeholders—professional practitioners, policy makers, managers, and administrators—so that more appropriate and effective programs and services can be formulated" (Stringer, 2014, p. 213). By disseminating action research findings, you can contribute to addressing complex educational issues. Schön (1983) describes the work of practitioner researchers as occupying "the swampy lowlands"—where problems of practice are messy and often lack clear, technical solutions. These problems "which are puzzling, troubling, and uncertain" (p. 40) are also of deep importance; they "are the problems of greatest human concern" (p. 42). It is crucial that action researchers share their knowledge in order to address critical problems confronting their fields.

There are also personal benefits to reporting on action research studies. According to Mills (2011), action researchers describe the process of sharing their insider knowledge as professionally rewarding, empowering, and validating. In writing up findings, action researchers create a product that highlights the hard work they have undertaken. Here, they enter into a larger academic community interested in generating and improving the knowledge base of practice. At the same time, "when asked to describe their methods of inquiry, they [practitioner researchers] speak of experience, trial and error, intuition, and muddling through" (Schön, 1983, p. 43). It can be a difficult process to document and sort through the complex work of action research. By following a series of steps, the writing process may seem more manageable.

Developing a Theory of Action

Perhaps most significant about the work of action researchers is the opportunity to develop **theories of action**. All too often we bemoan the gap between theory and practice—what is theorized seems to be impossible to fully implement in practice. Action research effectively closes the gap by describing what happens in practice. According to Parsons and Brown (2002), for teacher action researchers, "teaching decisions are not only shaped by theory and research, but in turn help give shape and new directions to educational theory and research" (p. 7). The findings from action research can be used to develop theories of action to describe what occurs when practices are implemented. These theories of action may result in improved practice and student performance. In other words, by describing how things work, action researchers provide guidance about how to avoid pitfalls common in practice and strategies to implement real change.

The emphasis here is not just on tacit or routine knowledge of practitioners but the knowledge that is developed through systematic and intentional reflection on practice. According to Altrichter, Feldman, Posch, and Somekh (2008), "in *reflection-in-action,* reflection distances itself from the flow of activities, interrupts it and focuses on data that represent the action in an objectified form" (italics in original, p. 274). In other words, the systematic approach to reflection enables the researcher to develop "objective" forms of knowledge or theories of action. These theories of action describe processes with a view to the data that defines those processes.

Critical forms of action research—those that interrogate the critical social and cultural issues that shape practice—can result in emancipatory change. Here, action researchers are concerned with democratic participation and alleviating oppression. Through critical action research, you can bring about positive social change by drawing attention to injustices, suggesting strategies for negotiating unequal power dynamics, and seeking deep change and enlightenment across communities of practice. The goal here is toward improving society.

Iterative Nature of Writing Up Findings

In what appears to be a recurring theme in action research, writing up findings is also an iterative process. A good starting point in the writing process is for action researchers to keep research journals. These journal entries can later be edited and combined with the data collected during the action research study to create a more holistic narrative.

The overall aim for the researcher is to communicate the purpose, findings, and significance of an action research project to outside readers in the final report. Below are step-by-step strategies for writing a formal action research report. For action researchers who do not intend to present their written findings to a larger audience, the writing process will nonetheless be a beneficial step in their reflection.

Regardless of the scope of the final report, it is recommended that action researchers do not wait until the very end of the project to begin writing. By keeping a running document throughout the project, action researchers can continuously and iteratively reflect on their research in writing. This may provide new insights about the research and make the task of writing a final report seem less daunting.

Strategies and Step-by-Step Guide for Writing Reports

There are many steps that action researchers can follow to develop a final report of the research. Since the aim is to clearly and succinctly describe the action research and its findings, it will be necessary to reduce a great deal of data into a narrative discussion about patterns with key examples. It will also be important to provide readers with the necessary contextual information to understand the factors that impacted the research. It will be helpful at the outset to consider the audience of your final report and to seek out a mentor text—a published action research report that you can emulate (see Activity 8A: Action Research Journal Search and Activity 8B: Evaluating Action Research Articles). As you begin to review action research articles, you will become more familiar with the genre of action research reporting and improve your ability to hone your messaging.

Introducing Your Study

Similar to other genres of educational research, action research reports begin with a broad overview of the study. This will provide readers with important background about the impetus for the study and the rationale for the action(s) pursued.

In the opening section of the research report, action researchers detail the problem(s) that led to the study. This includes providing background details about the context of the problem, including the setting, affected individuals or groups, and desired outcomes. Here, action researchers also refer to relevant research literature or other resources that informed the study. This provides a link between the current work and previous work. You can refer to anecdotal or baseline data that may have also inspired the study. Once the foundation of the study is described, you can go on to describe the goals of the study, including the desired action or experiential change that was pursued.

Methods and Data Collection Procedures

In addition to describing the action pursued, the final report details the methods used to collect data. This section provides other educators and researchers the ability to replicate the study for their own contexts. The section also provides information by which the reader can judge the appropriateness of the methods and the overall logic of the study. According to Avery (2008), it is "important that authors be vigilant about explaining their theoretical perspectives, methodologies, and research tools. . . . The findings and conclusions of research studies should enlighten us, but so too should the ways in which researchers conceptualize and implement their studies" (p. 8). Action researchers should provide details about the procedures followed, including the research questions posed, the amount and types of data collected, the process followed for collecting data, and the approach to analyzing data.

Organizing Evidence and Developing Assertions

The process of organizing evidence to develop assertions about the findings can be very challenging. Here, action researchers must examine the evidence collected across the study to identify patterns and to describe those patterns. Following the processes related to data analysis discussed in the previous chapters, action researchers can identify clear trends in the data and begin to develop assertions. Often action researchers will return in this section to the research questions that formed the basis of the study. A simple format for sharing findings is to address each research question with evidence collected from the study and an analytical discussion of the evidence. Another approach is to develop a list of assertions or statements about the results of the study. These can be expanded upon using specific examples from the data analysis.

Discussing the Significance of the Findings

Once the report outlines the major findings, the action researcher must help the reader make sense of the meaning and significance of those findings. Here, the action researcher returns to the questions originally posed to discuss the extent to which progress was made to solve the problem over the course of the study. Action researchers also return to the research literature to make connections between their findings and previous studies. Here, the literature will help provide terminology or language that can assist you in defining and describing what you have observed in the data.

In this section, action researchers also begin to make sense of their data by posing theories of action or theories about action. In other words, based on the findings and evidence collected, you make an argument about how and why phenomena and processes occur. You can then provide new theories to guide future action. The discussion of the findings is a crucial section of the final research report in that it provides action researchers with the opportunity to weigh in about the importance of their work and the significance of it relative to the larger educational community.

Proposing Additional Study

Of course, action research is never really completed. Rather, it is an ongoing process. Answering research questions related to practice leads to additional questions. In the final section of the report, action researchers outline proposals for future study. Here you can outline any unfinished or nagging issues raised by the present study and suggest additional lines of inquiry. This section, again, provides action researchers with a voice to weigh what they consider to be the most pressing issues still unsolved or unaddressed.

Proofreading and Editing

In order for research reports to make an impact, they must be understandable and well written. It is important to meet the writing conventions of the audience and to take the necessary time to proofread and edit the final copies of action research reports. In addition to editing your own work, hire an editor or recruit a friend to edit your text. Do not rely on the auto-correct features of your word processing software to catch errors. Also, it is important to consult style guides as necessary. Many educational researchers follow the American Psychological Association (APA) style format. It is important to double-check the style requirements, especially for those submitting action research reports for university courses or for publication in academic journals.

Generating Collaborative Action Research Reports

Action researchers working in groups have the benefit of collaborating with like-minded professionals who are also familiar with the problem under study. In some cases, group members may pursue individual action research studies about the same topic or they may conduct a study as a group. In the latter example, members should develop an accountability plan at the outset of a study to clarify the roles and expected contributions of each member of the group. The group dynamic will create a natural forum for sharing and testing ideas and conclusions about the findings of the study. According to Koshy (2010), "this [collaboration] makes it easier to seek common understandings and interpretations so the findings are more representative" (p. 120).

One difficulty in writing a collaborative action research report is determining the most appropriate voice. Whereas traditional educational research literature tends to aim toward an objective narrator, most action research adopts a subjective tone. In these reports, authors often refer to the researcher in the first person. For example, an action research project might describe a classroom-based project like this: "I noticed that my students were not actively engaged in our whole-class discussions on a regular basis, so I determined to integrate Paideia seminars." The emphasis here is on the *I*—representing the researcher as an active participant in the research process. Collaborative groups can adopt similar language to describe what *we* did in our study. However, there may be times when individual action researchers have experiences that diverge from the group. In such situations, group members must remain flexible in following formats that can most accurately represent the experiences of individual group members. Options include integrating anecdotes, vignettes, or referring to individuals by their first or last name—for example, "Although we all felt that Paideia seminar would be beneficial for our students, Mark, who teaches in an inclusion classroom, was particularly interested in integrating Paideia to engage his students with special needs." As long as authors keep in mind the needs of their audience members, there are limitless possibilities about the form of the final action research report.

Action Research Dissertations and Theses

Graduate students may choose to pursue action research to fulfill the requirements for a dissertation or thesis at their college or university. Since dissertations and theses serve as the final exam for graduate programs, most universities set explicit formatting requirements as well as implicit expectations regarding the scope and depth of the research. Often these requirements include "a higher degree of critical engagement with existing theory and literature and a greater depth of conceptual analysis" (Koshy, 2010, p. 131). It is important to clarify the requirements and expectations with your graduate advisor and committee members before undertaking an action research project. Once these expectations are set, you can follow the steps outlined in this text for posing problems, developing research questions, collecting and analyzing data, and presenting findings. A common format is the five-chapter dissertation, including the following: (1) introduction and discussion of the problem, (2) review of the literature, (3) research methods, (4) presentation of the findings, and (5) discussion of the findings and conclusions. Herr and Anderson's (2014) text specifically addresses the unique issues that occur in action research dissertations and can be an invaluable resource for graduate students. See also the appendix at the end of this chapter for an example rubric for an action research report.

edTPA Reports

Teacher candidates enrolled in preservice teacher education programs that require edTPA reports can follow a truncated version of the steps above for developing a final written report. According to Girtz (2014), "the notion of action" is similar in the edTPA protocol and in action research since "the primary mode of such action [is] teaching" (p. 79). Also, in both cases, "the results are continually evaluated and reflection then informs [the] following action steps" (p. 79). Of the five dimensions of the edTPA assessment, "analyzing teaching effectiveness" seems to align most closely with the inquiry stance of action research. By integrating action research into teacher education programs, especially its focus on inquiry and reflection, teacher educators can inculcate the habits of mind necessary for candidates to navigate the requirements of edTPA. The results of a larger action research project could also be part of the evidence presented to edTPA as part of the requirements for program completion. Another option may be to pursue the "shortcuts" highlighted across this text for honing your skills of systematic and intentional reflective inquiry (see also Activity 8C: Practice Writing Exercise).

Action Research as "Risky Business"

It is important for anyone interested in engaging in practitioner research to understand that this form of research is "risky business" (Lytle, 1993) for action researchers. According to Lytle (1993), "the consequences of 'telling the truth'—about oneself and one's students—often become particularly unsettling and even somewhat threatening when taking the data outside the group" (p. 23). These risks involve not only publicly acknowledging personal assumptions, misconceptions, and areas in need of improvement but also the risk of not being taken seriously by administrators or university researchers.

For guidance in navigating this "risky business," action researchers must rely on the ethical standards described in Chapter 2. These include maintaining high standards in the development of the research study and in reporting findings. For example, you must avoid making false claims about data or findings. In writing final reports, action researchers do not include details that may reveal the identity of participants. Efforts to preserve confidentiality include using pseudonyms when appropriate and keeping descriptive details as vague as possible to protect the identity of individuals and other entities.

As long as ethical standards for educational research are maintained throughout the process of the study, including in the development of the final report, the findings should be allowed to speak for themselves. It is hard to imagine just how much impact your study may have on another's practice. By putting your findings "out there," you may be taking a risk but you also are advocating for a topic about which you care deeply. Following the validation and legitimation processes described below will help you maintain high ethical standards for your research and ensure the trustworthiness of your work.

Ensuring Trustworthiness

Action researchers are responsible for ensuring that their findings are legitimate and based on evidence collected over the course of the study. In addition to ensuring the logic of your study (i.e., clear connections between research questions, methods and findings), there are several steps that you can take to ensure the trust-worthiness of your research findings. These include collecting data to **saturation**, triangulating data collection and analysis, and seeking critical feedback through **member checking**, critical friends, and **peer review**.

Saturation

Saturation refers to the process of collecting data until you reach a point by which you have thoroughly "saturated" the results. According to Namey and Trotter (2015), saturation means "that you 'interview to redundancy,' or collect data until you are no longer learning something new about the topic" (p. 448). In other words, as you collect and analyze data, you begin to encounter the same phenomenon over and over again (i.e., themes from interviews begin to repeat as you code transcripts) or you have collected as much data as is reasonably possible (you have interviewed all of the appropriate participants). Some researchers offer more specific guidance regarding saturation. For example, according to Fusch and Ness (2015),

> data saturation is reached when there is enough information to replicate the study (O'Reilly & Parker, 2012; Walker, 2012), when the ability to obtain additional new information has been attained (Guest et al., 2006), and when further coding is no longer feasible (Guest et al., 2006). (references in original, p. 1408)

Regardless of the approach to data collection you take, it is important to address the issue of saturation in your final research report. Readers are interested to learn how you determined the scope of your study, including the amount of data collected and the length of time.

Triangulation

Saturation can be achieved by collecting and analyzing data from multiple sources and in multiple ways—a process referred to as triangulation (refer to Chapter 5). Triangulation involves collecting data about a single topic through multiple approaches, including interviewing, observing, and document analysis. For example, a study about a classroom practice might include interviewing students, observing the students engaged in the classroom practice, and analyzing samples of student work as evidence of their outcomes of engaged classroom practice. Triangulation can also refer to using a variety of approaches to data analysis—for example, content analysis and open coding (see also Chapter 6).

Vetting Your Study

Saturation and triangulation are just two of many approaches that action research-ers can take to ensure the trustworthiness of their findings. Other strategies include vetting findings by seeking the opinions of key stakeholders through member checking, engaging critical friends groups, and undergoing peer review.

Member Checking

Member checking involves the process of going back to study participants and asking them to review transcripts or final reports to ensure the documents accurately capture their experiences. This can occur during the action research study or at its culmination. In order for member checking to be beneficial, action researchers must alert participants about the purposes of the action research study, the aim of member checking, and the overall desired outcomes. For example, participants can be encouraged to read for accuracy as well as to offer additional information or insight. Of course, action researchers must provide adequate time for participants to review the materials in order to receive helpful feedback.

Critical Friends

Critical friends groups are a natural feature of collaborative action research studies in which groups of peers engage in research about the same or similar topics. Solo action researchers should also seek out a group of critical friends either in person or online. Critical friends groups provide supportive and constructive feedback to ensure that the researcher has thoughtfully and logically pursued her research. Critical friends groups can take many forms. Koshy (2010) recommends establishing "validation meetings" with critical friends with insights relevant to the topic under study. In order to improve their relative effectiveness, it is important to seek out critical friends with a variety of perspectives. A school administrator may provide very different feedback than a fellow teacher or a parent.

Critical friends provide formative feedback throughout the research process, including during the formulation of research problems and research questions, development of data collection methods, analysis of the data, and generation of the findings. Critical friends can be invaluable in identifying issues of bias and subjectivity. They can also provide summative feedback about the "usefulness and replicability of your research" (Koshy, 2010, p. 120). Sharing action research with critical friends is one form of peer review.

Peer Review

More formal peer review occurs when action researchers submit their final reports for publication in journals or as proposals for conference presentations. Blind peer review provides an important outlet for the action research to be reviewed and evaluated by peers. Often editors of journals or conference organizers will include feedback from reviewers in decisions letters. This feedback can be invaluable in improving the final reports of action research studies. Addressing concerns about the validity of action research, Zeichner (1994) strongly advocates for peer review as a necessary tool to prevent the reification of "practices that are harmful to students and may undermine important connections between institutions and their communities" (p. 66). In other words, peer review provides a means for action researchers to check their assumptions and seek external feedback.

Alternatives to Traditional Written Reports

There may be situations where it is expedient for action researchers to pursue alternatives to formal written reports to describe their studies and findings. This may include creating a shorter research brief or a multimedia presentation that combines words and images to present the findings of a study. In one notable example, Stock (1993) adapted her action research study into a stage play, *The Bridge*, and included examples of student experiences collected over the course of her study. Of course, it is important to consider the audience when developing these reports or presentations.

Professional conferences provide a forum for action researchers to present their work and to receive feedback from discussants and/or audience members. There are a variety of types of conferences at the local, state, and national/international levels. Conferences can be practitioner-oriented or focused on empirical research. Most conferences are associated with professional groups and subject area specialties. Many of these professional groups offer discounts for student members. A good way to gauge the fit of your research for a conference is to browse online programs from previous conferences. These programs are usually available through the conference site or through the professional organization. Activity 8D: Developing Conference Proposals will lead you through the requisite steps for developing a proposal.

Social Media

Action researchers have a variety of opportunities to share their findings through web-based and social media outlets. You can self-publish your final research report through online blogging tools and other Web 2.0 applications. There are also many applications that make it easy to feature your research by producing and publishing your own website (Google Sites, Weebly, etc.). When determining the most appropriate format and tools for your final report, it is important to weigh the needs of your audience members. It is also important to consider the "reach" of the media you choose. For example, can you reach more teachers by publishing a blog or by creating a website? Also important is considering the affordances of various platforms for making an impact on practice. Can you attach additional resources such as links to readings, handouts, and the like that other practitioners can consult in addition to your work?

Advocating for Yourself and Others

Many action researchers report that the process of developing, implementing, and writing about a study is empowering. By refining their professional expertise using a methodology that is largely self-guided, action researchers take control of the knowledge domain. They direct the inquiry and frame the findings. They have the opportunity to take risks and make changes through the process of conducting action research. It is important that action researchers also take part in determining the impact of their work.

In addition to reporting findings through traditional means such as in professional publications or at professional conferences, you can become an advocate for the people and issues you studied. For example, Arlene, an action researcher who studied the outcomes of her African American male students, became an advocate for these students within her school community. She helped lead school-wide professional development sessions focused on culturally relevant instruction and developed collaborative relationships with ministers and parents from the communities in which her students lived. Her action research project raised her own awareness of the unique needs of these students within her classroom, which she then leveraged to improve their experiences across the school. Arlene worked with school administrators to reduce the number of disciplinary referrals her students received, and together they developed a plan to better support positive student behavior. The outcomes of her research went beyond merely researching student outcomes to understanding larger systems at work in her school. Through her own study, along with her review of relevant literature, she was able to make an impact on the school community.

Your advocacy work can range from small in scale and local, to broad and more holistic or widespread. As the action researcher, you have the opportunity and agency to determine the path that makes the most sense for you. You may decide to start small, by reaching out to colleagues and peers or seek out connections across institutions. Regardless of your approach, your work has value and can bring about change.

Seeking Allies

Today there is a growing awareness of the power of **collective impact**. This occurs when like-minded groups join together to pool resources to tackle a larger social issue. Often these groups are made up of people from organizations that each seek to address one aspect of the larger problem. For example, if childhood poverty is an issue confronting a community, groups that focus on child and maternal health, food resources, mental health, occupational training, housing, and/or education may all join together to provide a network of services to address child poverty and its effects. By pooling resources, the group capitalizes on individual strengths and expertise to make a bigger impact.

Although collective action was originally developed for large-scale projects and organizations with infrastructure already in place, action researchers can adapt the core conditions of collective impact to their own work. This involves communicating openly with collaborators to develop a common goal. While not everyone has to agree to the same perspective on an issue, there must be a common aim in mind. Similarly, developing shared measurement and data collection systems will be invaluable toward evaluating success.

Action researchers can take up a model of collective impact either as an outcome of their work or by developing collaborative action research groups. For example, you could join other action researchers studying a similar issue to create an advocacy group. Based on the findings of research conducted by individual members, your group could develop a collaborative strategic plan. Grade-level and departmental professional learning communities (PLCs) or professional learning teams (PLTs) provide a natural structure for such a team approach. For example, if teachers within a PLT each conducted action research, all with the aim of improving instruction, collectively the group could develop an action plan for improving instruction. Similarly, if a group of educators in a single school conducted action research related to classroom management and student behavior, they could work with a variety of advocacy groups to support positive student outcomes.

By seeking allies, action researchers can reduce the isolation that practitioners often face. Allies can be found within a single setting or across educational systems. By engaging community members, the impact of a single project can have ripple effects across an entire community.

Reflection

Although the steps presented here seem to take a fairly linear, objective approach to developing action research reports, action researchers should not be dissuaded from engaging in storytelling in their work. Stories and anecdotes can often provide powerful images to describe experiences. Action researchers should approach this work from a narrative perspective, to tell their story in a way that is accurate, meaningful, and engaging to the reader.

The work of action researchers may very well emerge from the "swampy lowlands" as Schön (1983) suggests. This means that action research is complex, messy, and often confusing or frustrating. Nonetheless, action research has great importance since it emerges from real issues related to everyday practice. It is only through tackling these issues, through systematic and intentional reflection, that strategies for solving problems of practice can emerge. Through careful attention to problem posing, data collection and analysis, and writing up findings, action research meets the conditions associated with the "rigor of relevance" (Schön, 1983).

This work is complex and significant. It is not likely to occur on the basis of a single action research study. Rather, action research becomes a tool in a larger commitment toward working for positive change. Once you have completed a first round of study, chances are new issues and questions will emerge. You will pursue these questions just as you previously initiated your original study, this time armed with your findings. Another round of study could expand on the original topic or take the research in an entirely new direction. Perhaps you can use a second round of study to rectify issues you faced in the past regarding data collection or analysis, or you could seek out a new set of participants. You are encouraged to take seriously your opportunity and responsibility as an action researcher to develop theories of action that make a positive impact on multiple layers of a community of practice.

CHAPTER SUMMARY

- Reflecting on practice is an essential feature of professional learning and development. Action research systemizes reflection by infusing it throughout the action research cycle.

- Reflection through writing provides action researchers with a voice, and writing about findings can also enhance the analytical work of researchers.

- It is crucial that action researchers share their knowledge in order to address crucial problems confronting the field.

- Action researchers can follow a series of steps to detail their studies and the major findings.

- The trustworthiness of an action research study is dependent on the logic of the study as well as the steps taken by the researcher to ensure trustworthiness, such as saturation, triangulation, member checks, critical friends, and peer review.

- Action research meets the "rigor of relevance" described by Schön (1983) in that it addresses the messy issues facing practitioners.

- Action researchers should feel empowered to not only share their findings but also build on their work through advocacy.

- Seeking out allies and stakeholders to engage in collective impact can reduce much of the isolation action researchers may experience in their daily practice.

SUGGESTED WEB-BASED RESOURCES

Writing Support

Purdue Online Writing Lab

https://owl.english.purdue.edu/owl/section/2/

Collaborative Action Research Network (CARN) (resources)

https://www.carn.org.uk/resources/

Action Research Journals

Action Research

http://journals.sagepub.com/home/arj

Educational Action Research

http://www.tandfonline.com/toc/reac20/current

Systematic Practice and Action Research

https://link.springer.com/journal/11213

International Journal of Action Research

http://www.hampp-verlag.de/hampp_e-journals_IJAR.htm

Professional Groups and Conferences

International Literacy Association

https://www.literacyworldwide.org/

International Society for Technology in Education

https://conference.iste.org/2018/

National Council of Teachers of English

http://www2.ncte.org/events/

National Council of Teachers of Mathematics

http://www.nctm.org/

National Council for the Social Studies

https://www.socialstudies.org/conference

National Science Teaching Association

http://www.nsta.org/conferences/

Collective Impact

Awareness. Action. Repeat.

https://awareactrepeat.weebly.com/

Collective Impact

https://ssir.org/articles/entry/collective_impact

QUESTIONS AND ACTIVITIES

Reflection Questions

1. Why is it important for action researchers to share their findings?

2. What might be some of the risks involved with sharing action research reports?

3. How can action researchers ensure the trustworthiness of their studies and their reports on findings?

4. What are available formats for action research reports? Which might be the best for your audience?

Practice Activities

Activity 8A: Action Research Journal Search

Search for action research journals that are available either online or in print. Look for their directions for author submissions. Choose one journal to answer the following questions about:

1. What is the scope of the journal?

2. What types of articles does the journal publish?

3. What are formatting requirements for the journal?

   a. Length, font, spacing

   b. Reference style (e.g., APA, MLA, Chicago Manual of Style)

   c. Artwork, figures, other graphics

   d. Other requirements?

Activity 8B: Evaluating Action Research Articles

Search for action research journals that are available either online or in print. Select one article from the journal archives that is relevant to your area of interest. Write a review of the article that includes a discussion of the following aspects of the article:

1. Purposes and rationale for the study

2. Methods

3. Findings

4. Formatting and organization

   Be sure to pay particular attention to the effectiveness of the final report. In your narrative you should highlight affordances and limitations of the author's approach.

Activity 8C: Practice Writing Exercise

In this exercise, you will collect data using a truncated format. The idea is to provide practice in quickly analyzing data by writing about it in narrative form. It would be ideal if you use this exercise to support your work in the action research project.

1. Create a short three- to four-question survey or interview protocol.

2. Deploy the survey or collect interview data from "participants."

3. Lay the data out on a table or desk and look for patterns.

4. Begin to write a narrative based on the patterns you see, using the following approach:

   a. Describe the pattern (this becomes your "finding").

   b. Describe evidence to support the pattern. Include specific examples from the data.

5. Edit/reorganize your narrative as you work your way through the data.

Activity 8D: Developing Conference Proposals

Search for a conference that matches your research interest. Identify when the conference will be held and what the requirements are for proposing a presentation for the conference. Develop a conference proposal based on your action research project that you will (or might) submit to the conference.

1. When and where will the conference be held?

2. When is the deadline for submitting a proposal?

3. What are the requirements for conference proposals?

4. Adapt your paper or topic idea to the proposal format on a separate page.

5. Submit your proposal (if applicable).

Activity 8E: Identifying Allies—External

Conduct a web-based search of local nonprofits and other groups that focus on areas of need similar to those that you identified in your research.

1. Are there any opportunities for collaboration?

2. How can you gain more information about their work?

3. How can you share what you know/have learned?

Activity 8F: Identifying Allies—Internal

Jot down a list of people within your organization that might be a good collaborator and ally as you move forward with your work. Plan a time to meet to discuss your research and possible future collective work. Develop a list of next steps and follow up within the month.

Activity 8G: Exploring Social Media Applications

Social media and Web 2.0 applications provide action researchers with opportunities to extend their work to larger audiences. Explore a variety of different types of Internet-based applications, such as Twitter, blogs, Facebook, wikis, or web authoring (e.g., Google Sites and WordPress).

1. How can you connect with other action researchers and advocacy groups through these applications?

2. Which application is best suited to your personal and professional goals?

APPENDIX

Final Action Research Report Rubric

This rubric can be adapted to a variety of settings. It can also provide guidance for planning the final research report.

	Possible Points	Points Awarded
Introduction and statement of the problem		
Research project fully described		
Question asked, problem identified, or areas of exploration clearly defined		
Thoughtful rationale provided, explains significance or importance of study		
Review of the literature		
Ideas drawn from published research, relevant theory, thoughtfully integrated into purpose, research design, analysis, and/or interpretation and discussion of findings		
Methodology		
Data collection methods are appropriate and clearly explained		
Data analysis methods are appropriate and clearly explained		
Findings		
Findings are accurately presented and supported by credible and trustworthy data		
Implications for one's practice (which emerged from findings) thoughtfully presented; clear explanation of what action researcher learned about his or her practice through conducting the research project		
Implications for others' practice (which emerged from the findings) thoughtfully presented		
Mechanics		
Research report carefully written in an interesting and readable style		
Proper APA format		
Total		

Comments:

References

Altrichter, H., Feldman, A., Posch, P., & Somekh, B. (2008). *Teachers investigate their work: An introduction to action research across the professions* (2nd ed.). New York, NY: Routledge.

Apple, M. (2005). *Educating the "right" way: Market, standards, God, and inequality*. New York, NY: Routledge.

Armento, B. (1991). Changing conceptions of research on the teaching of social studies. In J. Shaver (Ed.), *Handbook of research in social studies teaching and learning* (pp. 185–196). New York, NY: Macmillan.

Au, W. (2016). Meritocracy 2.0: High-stakes, standardized testing as a racial project of neoliberal multiculturalism. *Educational Policy, 30*(1), 39–62.

Aubusson, P., Ewing, R., & Francis, G. (2009). *Action learning in schools: Reframing teachers' professional learning and development*. New York, NY: Routledge.

Avery, P. G. (2008). From the editor. *Theory and Research in Social Education, 36*(1), 6–8.

Ballenger, C. (1996). Learning the ABCs in a Haitian preschool: A teacher's story. *Language Arts, 73*, 317–323.

Blackman, A., & Fairey, T. (2007). *The photovoice manual: A guide to designing and running participatory photography projects*. London, UK: Photo Voice.

Bolick, C. M., Torrez, C., & Manfra, M. M. (2014). History through a child's eye: Pre-service teachers making sense of children's understandings. *Social Studies Research and Practice, 9*(3), 1–20.

Boote, D. N., & Beile, P. (2005). Scholars before researchers: On the centrality of the dissertation literature review in research preparation. *Educational Research, 34*(6), 3–15.

Borko, H., Whitcomb, J., & Byrnes, K. (2008). Genres of research in teacher education. In M. Cochran-Smith, S. Feiman-Nemser, & D. J. McIntyre (Eds.), *Handbook of research on teacher education: Enduring questions in changing contexts* (3rd ed., pp. 1017–1049). New York, NY: Routledge.

Bouillion, L. M., & Gomez, L. M. (2001). Connecting school and community with science learning: Real world problems and school–community partnerships as contextual scaffolds. *Journal of Research in Science Teaching, 38*, 878–898.

Brause, R., & Mayher, J. S. (1991). *Search and re-search: What the inquiring teacher needs to know*. New York, NY: Falmer.

Burns, T. J. (2009). Searching for peace: Exploring issues of war with young children. *Language Arts, 86*, 421–430.

Capra, F. (1982). *The turning point: Science, society, and the rising culture*. New York, NY: Bantam.

Carr, A. A. (1997). User-design in the creation of human learning systems. *Educational Technology Research & Development, 45*(3), 5–22.

Carr, W., & Kemmis, S. (1986). *Becoming critical: Education, knowledge and action research*. London, UK: Falmer Press.

Catapano, S., & Song, K. H. (2006). Let's collaborate and infuse citizenship education: Kids voting in primary classrooms. *Social Studies Research and Practice, 1*(1), 55–66.

Charmaz, K. (2008). Constructionism and the grounded theory method. In J. A. Holstein & J. F. Gubrium (Eds.), *Handbook of constructionist research* (pp. 397–412). New York, NY: Guilford.

Charmaz, K. (2014). *Constructing grounded theory* (2nd ed.). Thousand Oaks, CA: Sage.

Cochran-Smith, M., & Lytle, S. L. (1993). *Inside and outside: Teacher research and knowledge*. New York, NY: Teachers College Press.

Cochran-Smith, M., & Lytle, S. L. (1999). The teacher research movement: A decade later. *Educational Researcher, 28*(7), 15–25.

Cochran-Smith, M., & Lytle, S. (2009). *Inquiry as stance: Practitioner research for the next generation*. New York, NY: Teachers College Press.

Corbin, J., & Strauss, A. (2008). *Basics of qualitative research: Techniques and procedures for developing grounded theory* (3rd ed.). Thousand Oaks, CA: Sage.

Corbin, J., & Strauss, A. (2015). *Basics of qualitative research: Techniques and procedures for developing grounded theory* (4th ed.). Thousand Oaks, CA: Sage.

Cornelissen, F., vanSwet, J., Beijaard, D., & Bergen, T. (2010). Aspects of school-university research networks that play a role in developing, sharing and using knowledge based on teacher research. *Teaching and Teacher Education, 27*, 147–156.

Creswell, J. W. (1994). *Research design: Qualitative and quantitative approaches.* Thousand Oaks, CA: Sage.

Creswell, J. W. (2013). *Qualitative inquiry and research design: Choosing among five approaches* (3rd ed.). Thousand Oaks, CA: Sage.

Creswell, J. W., & Plano, V. L. (2007). *Designing and conducting mixed methods research.* Thousand Oaks, CA: Sage.

Crotty, M. (1998). *The foundations of social research.* Thousand Oaks, CA: Sage.

Darling-Hammond, L. (2007). Race, inequality and educational accountability: The irony of "No Child Left Behind." *Race, Ethnicity, and Education, 10*(3), 245–260.

Delgado, R., & Stefanic, J. (2012). *Critical race theory: An Introduction* (2nd ed.). New York, NY: New York University Press.

Denzin, N. K., & Lincoln, Y. S. (Eds.). (2000). *Handbook of qualitative research* (2nd ed.). Thousand Oaks, CA: Sage.

Dewey, J. (1933). *How we think.* Boston, MA: D. C. Heath.

Dewey, J. (1938). *Experience and education.* New York, NY: Simon and Schuster.

Dey, I. (1993). *Qualitative data analysis: A user-friendly guide for social scientists.* New York, NY: Routledge.

DuFour, R., DuFour, R., Eaker, R., & Many, T. (2010). *Learning by doing: A handbook for professional learning communities at work* (2nd ed.). Bloomington, IN: Solution Tree.

DuFour, R., & Eaker, R. (1998). *Professional learning communities at work: Best practices for enhancing student achievement.* Alexandria, VA: Association for Supervision and Curriculum Development.

DuFour, R., & Fullan, F. (2013). *Cultures built to last. Systemic PLCs at work.* Bloomington, IN: Solution Tree.

Education Week. (2016). *Mindset in the classroom: A national study of K-12 teachers.* Bethesda, MD: Education Week Research Center. Retrieved from https://www.edweek.org/media/ewrc_mindsetinthe classroom_sept2016.pdf

Egbert, J., & Sanden, S. (2014). *Foundations of education research: Understanding theoretical components.* New York, NY: Routledge.

Eisner, E. (1992). The federal reform of schools: Looking for a silver bullet. *Phi Delta Kappan, 73*(9), 722–723.

Elliott, J. (1985). Facilitating action research in schools: Some dilemmas. In R. Burgess (Ed.), *Field methods in the study of education* (pp. 235–262). London, UK: Falmer.

Elliott J. (1991). *Action research for educational change.* Milton Keynes, UK: Open University Press.

Elliott, J. (2007). *Reflecting where the action is: The selected works of John Elliott.* New York, NY: Routledge.

Fairtest.org. (n.d.). *FairTest: The National Center for Fair and Open Testing.* Retrieved from http://www.fairtest.org/

Falk, B., & Blumenreich, M. (2005). *The power of questions: A guide to teacher and student research.* Portsmouth, NH: Heinemann.

Fecho, B. (2001). "Why are you doing this?" Acknowledging and transcending threat in a critical inquiry classroom. *Research in the Teaching of English, 36*(1), 9–37.

Forsey, M. (2012). Interviewing individuals. In S. Delamont (Ed.), *Handbook of qualitative research in education* (pp. 364–376). Cheltenham, UK: Edward Elgar.

Fusch, P. I., & Ness, L. R. (2015). Are we there yet? Data saturation in qualitative research. *The Qualitative Report, 20*(9), 1408–1416.

Gaurino, C. M., Reckase, M. D., & Wooldridge, J. M. (2015). Can value-added measures of teacher performance be trusted? *Education Finance and Policy, 10*(1), 117–156. Retrieved from http://www.mitpressjournals.org/doi/full/10.1162/EDFP_a_00153

Gay, G. (2002). *Culturally responsive teaching: Theory, research, and practice.* New York, NY: Teachers College Press.

Girtz, S. (2014). Ignatian pedagogy and its alignment with the new teacher bar exam (edTPA) and action research frameworks. *Jesuit Higher Education: A Journal, 3*(1), 75–80.

Gitlin, A., & Haddon, J. (1997). Educational research: Acting on power relations in the classroom. In

S. Hollingsworth (Ed.), *International action research* (pp. 70–84). London, UK: Falmer Press.

Glanz, J. (1999). A primer on action research for the school administrator. *Clearing House, 72,* 301–305.

Glaser, B. G., & Strauss, A. L. (1967). *The discovery of grounded theory: Strategies for qualitative research.* Chicago, IL: Aldine.

Glesne, C. (1999). *Becoming qualitative researchers* (2nd ed.). New York, NY: Addison Wesley Longman.

Gore, J. M., & Zeichner, K. M. (1991). Action research and reflective teaching in preservice teacher education: A case study from the United States. *Teaching & Teacher Education, 7,* 119–136.

Grimmett, P., & MacKinnon, A. (1992). Craft knowledge and the education of teachers. In G. Grant (Ed.), *Review of research in education* (pp. 385–456). Washington, DC: American Educational Research Association.

Guest, G., Bunce, A., & Johnson, L. (2006). How many interviews are enough? An experiment with data saturation and variability. *Field Methods, 18*(1), 59–82.

Guest, G., Namey, E., & Mitchell, M. L. (2013). *Collecting qualitative data: A field manual for applied research.* Thousand Oaks, CA: Sage.

Habermas, J. (1972). *Knowledge and human interest.* London, UK: Heinemann.

Hackenberg, A. J. (2010). Mathematical caring relations in action. *Journal for Research in Mathematics Education, 41,* 236–273.

Harris, D. N. (2011). *Value-added measures in education: What every educator needs to know.* Cambridge, MA: Harvard Education Press.

Hatch, T. (2006). Improving schools in turbulent times. *The New Educator, 2,* 267–276.

Hatch, T., & Shulman, L. S. (2005). *Into the classroom: Developing the scholarship of teaching and learning.* San Francisco, CA: Jossey-Bass.

Hendricks, C. (2009). Using action research to improve educational practices: Where we are and where are we going. *Journal of Curriculum and Instruction, 3*(1), 1–6.

Henning, J. E., Stone, J. M., & Kelly, J. L. (2009). *Using action research to improve instruction: An interactive guide for teachers.* New York, NY: Routledge.

Herr, K., & Anderson, G. (2014). *The action research dissertation: A guide for students* (2nd ed.). Thousand Oaks, CA: Sage.

Hyland, N. E., & Noffke, S. E. (2005). Understanding diversity through social and community inquiry: An action-research study. *Journal of Teacher Education, 56,* 367–381.

James, J. H. (2008). Teachers as protectors: Making sense of preservice teachers' resistance to interpretation in elementary history teaching. *Theory & Research in Social Education, 36,* 172–205.

Johnson, B., & Christensen, L. (2008). *Educational research: Quantitative, qualitative, and mixed approaches.* Thousand Oaks, CA: Sage.

Johnston, M. (2005). The lamp and the mirror: Action research and self studies in the social studies. In K. Barton (Ed.), *Research methods in social studies education: Contemporary issues and perspectives* (pp. 57–83). Greenwich, CT: Information Age.

Karp, J. A., & Brockington, D. (2005). Social desirability and response validity: A comparative analysis of overreporting voter turnout in five countries. *Journal of Politics, 67,* 825–840.

Kaufman, R. A., & English, F. W. (1979). *Needs assessment: Concept and application.* Englewood Cliffs, NJ: Educational Technology.

Kelley, L. (2006). Learning to question in kindergarten. *Social Studies Research and Practice, 1*(1), 45–54.

Kemmis, S., & Grundy, S. (1997). Educational action research in Australia: Organization and practice. In S. Hollingsworth (Ed.), *International action research: A casebook for educational reform* (pp. 40–48). London, UK: Falmer.

Kemmis, S., & McTaggart, R. (2007). Participatory action research: Communicative action and the public sphere. In N. Denzin & Y. Lincoln (Eds.), *Strategies of qualitative inquiry* (3rd ed., pp. 271–330). Thousand Oaks, CA: Sage.

Kincheloe, J. (1991). *Teachers as researchers: Qualitative inquiry as a path to empowerment.* London, UK: Falmer.

Kincheloe, J. (1995). Meet me behind the curtain: The struggle for a critical post-modern action research. In P. L. McLaren & J. M. Giarelli (Eds.), *Critical theory and educational research* (pp. 71–90). Albany: State University of New York Press.

Koshy, V. (2010). *Action research for improving educational practice* (2nd ed.). Thousand Oaks, CA: Sage.

Kowal, S., & O'Connell, D. C. (2014). Transcription as a crucial step of data analysis. In U. Flick (Ed.), *The SAGE handbook of qualitative data analysis* (pp. 64–79). London, UK: Sage.

Krueger, R. A., & Casey, M. A. (2009). *Focus groups: A practical guide for applied research* (4th ed.). Thousand Oaks, CA: Sage.

Kvale, S., & Brinkmann, S. (2009). *InterViews: Learning the craft of qualitative research interviewing*. Thousand Oaks, CA: Sage.

Ladson-Billings, G. (1998). What is critical race theory and what's it doing in a nice field like education? *International Journal of Qualitative Studies in Education, 11*(1), 7–24.

Ladson-Billings, G. (2009). *The Dreamkeepers: Successful teachers of African American children*. San Francisco, CA: Wiley.

Lagemann, E. C. (2000). *An elusive science: The troubling history of education research*. Chicago, IL: University of Chicago Press.

Lather, P. (1991). *Getting smart: Feminist research and pedagogy within the postmodern*. New York, NY: Routledge.

Lather, P. (1996). Troubling clarity: The politics of accessible language. *Harvard Educational Review, 66*(3), 525–545.

Levin, B. B, & Rock, T. C. (2003). The effects of collaborative action research on preservice and experienced teacher partners in professional development schools. *Journal of Teacher Education, 54*, 135–149.

Lewis, C., Guerrero, M., Makikana, L., & Armstrong, M. (2002, Spring). Exploring language identity, and the power of narrative. *Bread Loaf Teacher Network Magazine*, 8–10.

Lincoln, Y. (1998). From understanding to action: New imperatives, new criteria, new methods for interpretive researchers. *Theory and Research in Social Education, 26*(1), 12–29.

Lytle, S. (1993). Risky business. *Quarterly of the National Writing Project and the Center for the Study of Writing and Literacy, 25*(1), 20–23.

Lytle, S. L., & Cochran-Smith, M. (1994). Inquiry, knowledge, and practice. In N. S. Hollingsworth & H. Sockett (Eds.), *Teacher research and educational reform* (pp. 22–51). Chicago, IL: University of Chicago Press.

Macintyre, C. (2000). *The art of action research in the classroom*. London, UK: David Fulton.

MacLean, M. S., & Mohr, M. (1999). *Teacher-researchers at work*. Berkeley, CA: National Writing Project.

Manfra, M. M. (2009). Action research: Exploring the theoretical divide between practical and critical approaches. *Journal of Curriculum and Instruction, 3*(1), 32–46.

Marshall, C., & Rossman, G. B. (2016). *Designing qualitative research* (6th ed.). Thousand Oaks, CA: Sage.

Martell, C. C. (2015). Learning to teach culturally relevant social studies: A White teacher's retrospective self-study. In P. Chandler (Ed.), *Doing race in social studies: Critical perspectives* (pp. 41–60). New York, NY: Information Age.

McCutcheon, G., & Jung, B. (1990). Alternative perspectives on action research. *Theory Into Practice, 29*(3), 144–51.

McKernan, J. L. (1996). *Curriculum action research: A handbook of methods and resources for the reflective practitioner*. London, UK: Kogan Page.

McKillip, J. (1987). *Needs analysis: Tools for the human services and education*. Thousand Oaks, CA: Sage.

McNiff, J. (2016). *You and your action research project* (4th ed.). New York, NY: Routledge.

McNiff, J., & Whitehead, J. (2010). *You and your action research project* (3rd ed.). New York, NY: Routledge.

Merriam, S. B. (2009). *Qualitative research: A guide to design and implementation*. San Francisco, CA: Jossey-Bass.

Merrow, J. (2001). *Choosing excellence: "Good enough" schools are not good enough*. Lanham, MD: Scarecrow.

Mertler, C. A. (2014). *Action research: Improving schools and empowering educators* (4th ed.). Thousand Oaks, CA: Sage.

Miles, M. B., Huberman, A. M., & Saldana, J. (2014). *Qualitative data analysis: A methods sourcebook* (3rd ed.). Thousand Oaks, CA: Sage.

Miller, S. M., Nelson, M. W., & Moore, M. T. (1998). Caught in the paradigm gap: Qualitative researchers' lived experience and the politics of epistemology. *American Educational Research Journal, 35*(3), 377–416.

Mills, G. E. (2011). *Action research: A guide for the teacher researcher* (4th ed.). Boston, MA: Pearson.

Mitchell, K., & Elwood, S. (2012). From redlining to benevolent societies: The emancipatory power of spatial thinking. *Theory and Research in Social Education, 40*(2), 134–163.

Moore, C. M. (1987). *Group techniques for idea building.* Newbury Park, CA: Sage.

Morgan, D. L. (1998). Practical strategies for combining qualitative and quantitative methods: Applications to health research. *Qualitative Health Research, 8*(3), 362–376.

Morgan, D. L., & Morgan, R. K. (2009). *Single-case research methods for the behavioral and mental health sciences.* Thousand Oaks, CA: Sage.

Namey, E., & Trotter, R. (2015). Qualitative research methods. In G. Guest & E. Namey (Eds.), *Public health research methods* (pp. 443–482). Thousand Oaks, CA: Sage.

Nichols, S. L., Glass, G. V., & Berliner, D. C. (2005). *High-stakes testing and student achievement: Problems for the No Child Behind Act.* Tempe, AZ: Education Policy Studies Laboratory. Retrieved from http://epsl.asu.edu/epru/documents/EPSL-0509-105-EPRU.pdf

Noddings, N. (1996). An ethic of caring and its implications for instructional arrangements. *American Journal of Education, 96*(2), 215–230.

Noffke, S. E. (1997). Professional, personal, and political dimensions of action research. In M. W. Apple (Ed.), *Review of research in education: Vol. 22* (pp. 305–343). Washington, DC: American Educational Research Association.

O'Reilly, M., & Parker, N. (2012, May). Unsatisfactory saturation: A critical exploration of the notion of saturated sample sizes in qualitative research. *Qualitative Research Journal,* 1–8.

Painter, D. D. (2004). *Teacher-research at Deer Park School.* Retrieved from www.fcps.k12.va.us/DeerParkES/TR/tchrch.htm

Park, P., Brydon-Miller, M., Hall, B., & Jackson, T. (1993). *Voices of change: Participatory research in the United States and Canada.* Westport, CT: Bergin & Garvey.

Parsons, R. D., & Brown, K. S. (2002). *Teacher as reflective practitioner and action researcher.* Belmont, CA: Wadsworth/Thomson Learning.

Patton, M. Q. (2015). *Qualitative research and evaluation methods: Integrating theory and practice* (4th ed). Thousand Oaks, CA: Sage.

Persson, M., & Solevid, M. (2014). Measuring political participation: Testing social desirability bias in a web-survey experiment. *International Journal of Public Opinion, 26*(1), 98–112.

Plummer, K. (2011). Critical humanism and queer theory: Living with the tensions. In N. K. Denzin & Y. S. Lincoln (Eds.), *The SAGE handbook of qualitative research* (4th ed., pp. 208–211). Thousand Oaks, CA: Sage.

Price, J. N. (2001). Action research, pedagogy, and change: The transformative potential of action research in pre-service teacher education. *Journal of Curriculum Studies, 33*(1), 43–74.

Rand Education. (2012). *Teachers matter: Understanding teachers' impact on student achievement.* Santa Monica, CA: RAND Corporation. Retrieved from http://www.rand.org/pubs/corporate_pubs/CP693z1-2012-09.html

Rearick, M., & Feldman, A. (1999). Orientations, product, reflections: A framework for understanding action research. *Teaching and Teacher Education, 15,* 333–349.

Reason, P., & Bradbury, H. (2001). *Handbook of action research: Participative inquiry and practice.* Thousand Oaks, CA: Sage.

Reinharz, S. (1992). *Feminist methods in social research.* New York, NY: Oxford University Press.

Rockoff, J. E. (2003). *The impact of individual teachers on student achievement: Evidence from panel data.* Cambridge: MA: Harvard University. Retrieved from http://files.eric.ed.gov/fulltext/ED475274.pdf

Rogers, D. L., Noblit, G. W., & Ferrell, P. (1990). Action research as an agent for developing teachers' communicative competence. *Theory Into Practice, 24,* 179–184.

Roulston, K. (2010). Considering qualitative in qualitative interviewing. *Qualitative Research, 19*(2), 199–228.

Rowell, L., Riel, M., & Polush, E. (2016). Defining action research: Situating diverse practices within varying frames of inquiry, science and action. In L. Rowell, C. Bruce, J. Shosh, & M. Riel (Eds), *Palgrave interactional handbook of action research* (pp. 1–13). New York, NY: Palgrave.

Saldaña, J. (2016). *The coding manual for qualitative researchers* (3rd ed.). Thousand Oaks, CA: Sage.

Schatzman, L., & Strauss, A. (1973). *Field research strategies for a natural society.* Englewood Cliffs, NJ: Prentice-Hall.

Schön, D. (1983). *The reflective practitioner.* New York, NY: Basics Books.

Schwandt, T. A. (1989). Recapturing moral discourse in evaluation. *Educational Researcher, 18*(8), 11–16, 34.

Schwandt, T. A. (2000). Three epistemological stance for qualitative inquiry: Interpretivism, hermeneutics, and social constructionism. In N. K. Denzin & Y. S. Lincoln (Eds.), *Handbook of qualitative research* (2nd ed., pp. 189–213). Thousand Oaks, CA: Sage.

Seidman, I. (2006). *Interviewing as qualitative research: A guide for researchers in education and the social sciences* (3rd ed.). New York, NY: Teachers College Press.

Shulman, L. S. (1987). Knowledge and teaching: Foundations of the new reform. *Harvard Educational Review, 57*(1), 1–21.

Somekh, B. (2010). The Collaborative Action Research Network: 30 years of agency in developing educational action research. *Educational Action Research, 18*(1), 103–121.

Stenhouse, L., Verma, G. K., Wild, R. D., & Nixon, J. (1982). *Teaching about race relations: Problems and effects.* London, UK: Routledge and Kegan Paul.

Stewart, A. J. (1994). Towards a feminist strategy for studying women's loves. In C. E. Franz & A. J. Stewart (Eds.), *Women creating lives: Identities, resilience and resistance* (pp. 11–35). Boulder, CO: Westview.

Stock, P. L. (1993). The function of anecdote in teacher research. *English Education, 25*(3), 173–187.

Strauss, A. (1987). *Qualitative analysis for social scientists.* New York, NY: Cambridge University Press.

Stringer, E. T. (2014). *Action research* (4th ed.). Thousand Oaks, CA: Sage.

Thornton, S. J. (2001). Educating the educators: Rethinking subject matter and methods. *Theory Into Practice, 40*(1), 72–79.

Tom, A. (1984). *ReDesigning teacher education.* Albany: State University of New York Press.

Tyson, C. A. (1986). A response to "Coloring epistemologies: Are our qualitative research epistemologies racially biased?" *Educational Researcher, 27*(9), 21–22.

van Manen, M. (1975). An exploration of alternative research orientations in social education. *Theory and Research in Social Education, 3*(1), 1–28.

van Manen, M. (1990). Beyond assumptions: Shifting the limits of action research. *Theory Into Practice, 29,* 152–157.

Van Someren, M. W., Barnard, Y. F., & Sandberg, J. A. (1994). *The think aloud method: A practical guide to modelling cognitive processes.* London, UK: Academic Press.

von Bertalanffy, L. (1968). *General systems theory.* New York, NY: Braziller.

Wade, R. C. (1999). Voice and choice in a university seminar: The struggle to teach democratically. *Theory & Research in Social Education, 27,* 70–92.

Walker, J. L. (2012). The use of saturation in qualitative research. *Canadian Journal of Cardiovascular Nursing, 22*(2), 37–46. Retrieved from http://www.cccn.ca

Watson, K. (2005). Queer theory. *Group Analysis, 38*(1), 67–81.

Weedon, C. (1997). *Feminist practice and poststructuralist theory* (2nd ed.). Oxford, UK: Blackwell.

Willig, C. (2014). Interpretation and analysis. In U. Flick (Ed.), *The SAGE handbook of qualitative analysis* (pp. 136–150). London, UK: Sage.

Wolcott, H. F. (1994). *Transforming qualitative data: Description, analysis, and interpretation.* Thousand Oaks, CA: Sage.

Zeichner, K. (1994). Personal transformation and social reconstruction through action research. In S. Hollingsworth & H. Sockett (Eds.), *Teacher research and educational reform* (pp. 66–85). Chicago, IL: University of Chicago Press.

Zeni, J. (2001). A guide to ethical decision making for insider research. In J. Zeni (Ed.), *Ethical issues in practitioner research* (pp. 153–165). New York, NY: Teachers College Press.

Index